The FRENCH
SLOW COOKER

*Beef Stew with Mushrooms,
Rosemary, and Tomatoes (page 86)*

The FRENCH SLOW COOKER

Michele Scicolone

PHOTOGRAPHS BY ALAN RICHARDSON

HOUGHTON MIFFLIN HARCOURT
BOSTON NEW YORK 2012

To Charles Scicolone—
and our next forty years together

Copyright © 2012 by Michele Scicolone
Photographs copyright © 2012 by Alan Richardson

For information about permission to reproduce selections from this book,
write to Permissions, Houghton Mifflin Harcourt Publishing Company,
15 Park Avenue South, New York, New York 10003.

www.hmhbooks.com

Library of Congress Cataloging-in-Publication Data
Scicolone, Michele.
The French slow cooker / Michele Scicolone ;
photographs by Alan Richardson.
    p. cm.
Includes index.
ISBN 978-0-547-50804-7
1. Electric cooking, Slow. 2. Cooking, French. 3. Cookbooks. I. Title.
TX827.S357 2011
641.5944—dc23   2011028601

Book design by Kris Tobiassen
Food styling by Anne Disrude
Prop styling by Betty Alfenito
Cover photograph: Bouillabaisse, page 122

Printed in the United States of America
DOC 10 9 8 7 6 5 4 3 2 1

Acknowledgments

After I wrote *The Italian Slow Cooker* a couple of years ago, I heard from many readers who told me how much they were enjoying the recipes and asked me to write another book like it. They made suggestions, sent me their best slow-cooking tips, asked thought-provoking questions, reviewed the book on their blogs, and inspired and encouraged me to write this book. Many thanks to all my readers for their kind comments. This book is for you!

It was a pleasure to work with everyone at Houghton Mifflin Harcourt once again, especially Rux Martin, my enthusiastic editor, who has a knack for understanding what I want to say and helps me find the right words to express my thoughts. This book has also benefited from the careful attention of production editor Rebecca Springer, and Kris Tobiassen created the striking design. Brittany Edwards, Tim Mudie, and other HMH staff members who work behind the scenes contributed much to this book as well, and I thank them for their hard work.

My grateful appreciation goes to my agent and friend, Judith Weber, who, with her love for good food of all kinds and French food in particular, lent this project her support and lots of good ideas.

For the glorious food photography, my thanks to Alan Richardson, who once again captured the deliciousness of slow-cooked food with his camera. Anne Disrude, the food stylist, never ceases to amaze me with her ability to make my dishes look mouthwatering. Betty Alfenito has an unerring eye when it comes to presentation, and her styling of the photos adds warmth and charm.

The one person I can always turn to whether I need an honest opinion, a helping hand, a big laugh, or some good wine is my husband, Charles. Thank you for sharing it all with me.

Mussels in Fennel and Tomato Broth (page 121)

Contents

Introduction... 1

Why a Slow Cooker? 3

Choosing a Slow Cooker 5

Tips and Techniques 7

Slow Cooker Safety 11

The French Pantry 13

SOUPS... 20

CHICKEN, TURKEY, AND DUCK 42

MEATS 76

SEAFOOD 118

SOUFFLÉS, QUICHES, AND OTHER EGG DISHES................................132

VEGETABLES 150

LEGUMES AND GRAINS 170

DESSERTS 188

BASICS...215

Index 225

Introduction

A few years ago, a friend and I decided to make cassoulet, a bean and meat stew that is an icon of French home cooking. We found a classic recipe and followed the instructions step by step. It took days to prepare, as we marinated the meat, simmered the stock and beans, sautéed the lamb, and finally baked everything all together. In between, we scrubbed a mountain of pots and pans. When it was finished, we had a memorable dinner party. It was a lot of fun and a lot of work, and neither of us ever attempted it again—until I decided to make the dish in my slow cooker.

I began by preparing a classic French stock, a rich dark beef broth that is the luxurious underpinning of many of the country's traditional dishes (store-bought beef broth works too). I put the beans on to soak the night before. Because the lamb, sausage, and duck would simmer together for many hours, no marinating was needed. I browned the onions in a little bacon fat and transferred them to the slow cooker. I added the beans, sausage, and other meats, pressed the start button, and went out, leaving my cassoulet to bubble away all day.

When I got home, I closed my eyes and inhaled. I felt as if I had arrived at the farmhouse kitchen of the French *grand-mère* I never had. During the cooking, the meat and beans had soaked up the flavors of the garlic and herbs. The cassoulet was hearty and soul-satisfying, with flavors as deep and delicious as my from-scratch version.

With the help of a slow cooker, it's easy to make homey and inexpensive French food in any kitchen. If you can make soup, stew, or pot roast, why not make them with a little French flair? Like cassoulet, the recipes in this book are not five-star restaurant haute cuisine. This is the kind of food you would enjoy in the kitchen of a good French home cook, or possibly a superstar chef on his or her day off.

People sometimes tell me that they are intimidated by the idea of French cooking. They think that they will need special equipment or rare ingredients. They are turned off by the thought of flambéing or food that looks like it came out of a science lab. Well, so am I! The ingredients in these recipes are available in well-stocked supermarkets, and I've included easily found alternates for the few less common items.

With rich homemade broth in my freezer, I have money in the bank for classical soups like Two-Way Potato-Leek (page 30) or Beef Stew with Mushrooms, Rosemary, and Tomatoes (page 86).

But the slow cooker comes into its own not only with soups and stews but with any number of French dishes that benefit from gentle, even heat. Soufflés and quiches are two foods that I adore, but cooked in the oven, they require careful timing and attention. While they puff in the gentle heat of the slow cooker, I can relax and enjoy my company and not have to worry about split-second timing. Now my soufflés are both beautiful to behold and as tender and delicate as an oven-baked soufflé. My slow cooker also makes moist, creamy quiches. I leave out the crust, so they are healthier and easier to make than their oven-baked cousins—and just as delicious.

Even fish and seafood do well in the slow cooker. Sturdy varieties like halibut, salmon, or grouper and shellfish such as scallops or shrimp are the best choices, since they poach gently without breaking apart. When company is coming, I often use the slow cooker to make the hearty fish stew Bouillabaisse (page 122), flavored with tomatoes, saffron, and herbs, and serve it with toasted bread and roasted pepper rouille. On weeknights when time is short, I simply slow cook some salmon fillets with Dijon mustard, a meal that is practically effortless, and if I have leftovers, they make a fine cold luncheon salad the next day—two healthy meals for the work of one.

The slow cooker also does a great job with vegetable dishes like gratins. Layered with herbs and seasonings and topped with melted cheese, the vegetables become imbued with delicate flavors and turn meltingly tender, sufficient for a meal with a green salad. And with the slow cooker, you can make pâtés as good as those created by any French chef. Whether it is a coarse and garlicky country pâté or a light and silky smooth chicken liver mousse, a pâté is perfect for a summer party, when no one wants to turn on the oven.

The slow cooker makes some of the best versions of satiny crème caramel, fudgy flourless chocolate cake, and homey bread pudding that I have ever eaten. Even crème brûlée comes out perfectly. (For the proper crunchy topping, I just run it under the broiler for a minute or so before serving.)

WHY A SLOW COOKER?

Wouldn't it be nice to have a kitchen assistant to do the cooking so that you could do more important things—like relax! Could you sometimes use another oven? How about a buffet or hot-beverage server for holiday parties or for days when family members arrive home at different times?

A slow cooker is all these things and more. Here are a few reasons every kitchen should have one.

≫ A slow cooker lets you make dishes when it suits your schedule. The cooker can be set for overnight, or while you are out, or when you are at home doing other things.

≫ A slow cooker saves money by using less energy than the oven or stovetop.

≫ Inexpensive cuts of meat fare best in a slow cooker, turning into succulent comfort food.

≫ Slow-cooked food tastes even better the next day, so you can cook once and prepare several meals, saving both time and money.

≫ A slow cooker is perfect for entertaining. You can enjoy your company while the slow cooker does all the work, or use your slow cooker as a buffet server to keep food or beverages warm.

≫ A slow cooker doesn't heat up the whole house like a conventional stove, so you won't mind using it on a hot summer day.

≫ A slow cooker is handy for cooking where ovens are not available, such as in a vacation home or on a boat.

Although the slow cooker gives results that are *magnifique,* it does not cook in exactly the same way as the stovetop or oven. For example, classic French recipes often call for generous amounts of both fresh and dried herbs, such as thyme, rosemary, or bay leaf. But in the slow cooker, dried herbs can become strong and overpowering, while fresh herbs turn tasteless. For that reason, I reduce the amount of dried herbs called for in traditional recipes. With fresh herbs, I find that I can get the flavor I want by adjusting the seasoning and stirring in a little more shortly before the end of the cooking time.

Other simple French kitchen techniques are perfectly applicable to the slow cooker, such as adding bread crumbs to some stews as a thickener instead of flour or cornstarch. (This works especially well with bean stews.) A squeeze or two of tomato paste from a tube is all it takes to enhance the color and flavor of soups and stews.

Much as I love the slow cooker's ability to save me work, I sometimes brown meats and vegetables before adding them to the slow cooker. Browning softens the texture, adds color, and enhances and deepens the flavors of the finished dish. But it is not absolutely essential, and you can skip that step if you prefer. French cooks don't always brown foods, and there are many times when browning is not only unnecessary but is, in fact, undesirable. For example, in a traditional White Veal Stew (page 94), the meat is not browned, so it remains delicate in taste and creamy white. Similarly, in Bargemen's Beef Stew (page 81), the cubes of beef are not browned, ensuring that the meat will be very tender. Chicken turns out just as moist and flavorful without browning.

With the help of my slow cooker, I can make fabulous feasts any day of the week that would be the envy of any French cook. Whether it's a seafood soup like bouillabaisse, a delicate soufflé, or a classic cassoulet I crave, I no longer have to wait for a special occasion or set aside hours to prepare it. I can assemble the dish and rely on my slow cooker to do all of the cooking for me whether I am at home or away. At the end of a long day, there is nothing more welcoming than coming home to a house filled with mouthwatering aromas and the comfort of a delicious dinner ready and waiting.

Choosing a Slow Cooker

If you are new to the slow cooker or have an older model, you should know that the slow cooker has come a long way since the prototypes of the 1970s. Those harvest gold, flame, or olive green pots caused a sensation, but they came in only one size and were extremely difficult to clean, because the crockery lining was not removable. Cooks tended to stick with basic recipes like chili and stew, and many of us thought that was all the appliances were good for.

Today's slow cooker models are available in all different sizes and have lots of features, such as removable inserts, programmable timers, and digital readouts. They are much more convenient and reliable than the early models and can handle far more complex recipes than could their predecessors.

Both first-timers and slow cooker veterans thinking of upgrading often ask me which slow cooker brand or model I prefer. Of the seven different slow cookers I used to test the recipes for this book, each one is a little bit different.

So what should you buy? Here are the essentials to look for.

> » A large-capacity cooker that can handle roasts, stews, cakes, or a big batch of soup. (All the recipes in this book were tested in a 5½-quart or larger slow cooker.)

> » A removable insert for easy cleaning and serving.

> » A glass cover that allows you to see how the food is cooking without lifting the lid.

> » A heatproof handle on the lid so that you don't need to use a pot holder when removing it.

» High, low, and warm temperature settings. The warm setting is perfect for those times when you want your cooker to double as a buffet server.

» A programmable timer that switches to the warm setting when the cooking time is finished.

» A signal light that shows at a glance when the cooker is operating.

» A beeper that sounds when the cooking time is up.

As manufacturers continue to add new features, slow cookers are becoming more versatile. Here are some features that are nice but not really necessary.

» A preprogrammed 1-hour high setting that brings food up to a safe cooking temperature quickly, then switches automatically to whatever setting you prefer.

» An insert that can be used on the stovetop or in the oven for browning and then go back into the slow cooker.

» A temperature probe.

» Lines on the inside of the insert marking the volume.

» An easy-to-read digital display.

» Extended cooking capability of up to 26 hours.

» Preprogrammed cookers. Press "beef stew" or another preset timing for a recipe, or set the timer manually.

» Multiple-size or adjustable inserts for large, medium, and small batches of food.

Tips and Techniques

Sure, you can toss a bunch of ingredients into a slow cooker and walk away. But if you want to make really delicious food, use the best ingredients, take the time to understand how your cooker operates, and learn a few handy techniques.

TIMING TIPS

» For many of the dishes in this book, a little more or less cooking time won't make a big difference: just use the indications in the recipe to see if the food is done.

» Slow cookers can vary in the way they cook. Newer models manufactured in the past decade or so are preset to cook hotter and faster than older models because of food safety concerns. The capacity of the cooker, the design, and the quantity, temperature, and shape of the ingredients can also influence the cooking time. If you have any doubts about doneness, check that the food has reached a safe temperature by using an instant-read thermometer (see box).

Always measure roasts and chicken in the thickest part, or in the center of the pot. Open the cover, stick the thermometer into the food, and quickly close the cover again. Wait a minute or so to allow the thermometer to register the temperature. The USDA suggests the following guidelines for safe temperatures for slow-cooked foods:

Chicken, turkey, and other poultry ....165°F
Pork, beef, and lamb stews and roasts...145°F
Ground meats, meat loaf, and pâté...165°F

» Chopped onions, carrots, and celery often taste better when they are softened first in a little oil or butter.

» Vegetables, especially roots like carrots, potatoes, and turnips, cook more slowly than meats, so for stews or soups that combine both, cut the vegetables into even pieces and place them in the bottom of the cooker.

» Chicken on the bone is less likely to overcook than boneless chicken. For white-meat chicken pieces, leave the skin on to help keep the meat moist as it cooks. For dark-meat pieces such as thighs and legs, remove the skin for a less fatty dish.

» Tougher, bone-in cuts of meat are generally the best choice for slow cooking. Not only do they hold up better during the long, slow cooking and turn out moist and delicious, they are also less expensive.

» Trim off visible fat from meats and chicken before cooking.

» Browning chicken is not necessary unless you are trying to jump-start the cooking. Browned or not, the bird will come out tasting and looking pretty much the same.

» Dried herbs and whole spices like bay leaves, thyme, and cinnamon sticks tend to become stronger-tasting during slow cooking, while fresh or frozen herbs lose flavor. Use less of the dried herbs and refresh them, if needed, by stirring in a little extra near the end of the cooking time.

» Fresh flat-leaf parsley adds bright flavor without being overwhelming and livens up the color of finished dishes, making food look more appealing.

» To keep delicate foods like tender vegetables or seafood from overcooking, add them toward the end of the cooking time.

» When seasoning soups or sauces, remember that store-bought broth can be very salty. If you use it instead of homemade broth, take the salt content into account.

» Liquid does not evaporate from the slow cooker, so you may need to thicken soups and stews. There are several ways to do this. The easiest is to turn the temperature to high and uncover the cooker for the last half hour or so to allow some of the liquid to evaporate. Or you can transfer some of the liquid to a saucepan and bring it to a boil on the stovetop until it reduces and thickens. Alternatively, bring the liquid in the saucepan to a simmer, then for every cup of liquid, stir together 1 tablespoon cornstarch or flour and 2 tablespoons cool water until smooth. Stir this mixture into the simmering liquid and cook for several minutes, until slightly thickened. Some soups or stews, especially those made with beans, can be thickened with bread crumbs. Use plain, unflavored bread crumbs from French bread, if possible, or panko (Japanese bread crumbs). Stir in as much as you need to thicken the liquid and cook for a few minutes longer to blend the flavors.

» Skim off the fat from the surface of cooked foods before serving.

EQUIPMENT TIPS

» For easier cleanup, spray the inside of the slow cooker with nonstick cooking spray before adding ingredients.

» For the best heat distribution, fill the cooker only half to two-thirds full.

» Try not to open the lid during the cooking if you can avoid it, because a slow cooker loses a lot of heat when you do that. If you do open it, add a little extra time—say, 20 minutes per peek—to the total cooking time.

» Before making a recipe that will be cooked in a bowl, a cake or loaf pan, ramekins, or a baking dish, make sure the dish fits in the insert of your slow cooker. It may have the right capacity, but if it has a wide rim or handles, it might not fit. Most large cookers (5½- to 7-quart capacity) can accommodate a 6 cup soufflé dish, four ramekins or custard cups, or a 7-inch springform pan. (You can find these at cookware shops or online.)

» A baking rack allows the heat to circulate around the pan or baking dish. You can buy a small rack, if need be, or improvise by crushing a sheet of aluminum foil into a ring shape and placing it in the bottom of the insert.

Slow Cooker Safety

SLOW COOKERS ARE SAFE. Since a slow cooker uses only about as much electricity as a 75-watt lightbulb, you can leave it on while you sleep or are out. Be aware that the outer surface may become hot, and always clear the countertop around the slow cooker. Don't plug other appliances into the same outlet, and never use an extension cord.

DEFROST FROZEN FOODS BEFORE PUTTING THEM IN THE SLOW COOKER. Otherwise, they may not reach a safe cooking temperature within 2 hours, the time that experts say is necessary to prevent the growth of bacteria.

DO NOT USE THE SLOW COOKER TO REHEAT COLD FOODS. Reheat foods on the stovetop to ensure that they reach a safe temperature as quickly as possible.

USE AN INSTANT-READ THERMOMETER to test the temperature of cooked foods.

IN THE EVENT OF A POWER OUTAGE WHILE YOU ARE AWAY, discard the food in the slow cooker even if it looks done. If an outage should occur while you are at home, transfer the food to the stovetop or an outdoor grill to finish cooking.

The French Pantry

CHEESE

From the tangy, herbal goat cheeses of Provence to the creamy cow's-milk cheeses of Brittany and Normandy and plenty of sheep's-milk cheeses in between, France offers an amazing and delectable variety of *fromages*. The best way to explore them is to find a good cheesemonger and take his or her advice until you find those that you like.

For cooking purposes, I have stuck with familiar varieties you are most likely to find in the United States. Of course, you can substitute similar cheeses if you like.

Emmental is a semi-firm cow's-milk cheese made primarily in Switzerland and France. A creamy yellow color, Emmental is nutty and flavorful without being sharp. A good all-purpose cheese, Emmental can be used in omelets, salads, and grilled cheese sandwiches.

Bleu d'Auvergne is buttery and milder than other blue cheeses. This cow's-milk cheese is delicious when crumbled over a salad, paired with apples or pears, or used as a topping for a burger. Roquefort, Gorgonzola, or Maytag Blue are good too.

Gruyère is a firm cow's-milk cheese. Although the flavor is similar to Emmental, Gruyère is earthier and more complex and does not have big holes. Gruyère melts beautifully, so it is perfect on top of onion soup, in a fondue, or as a grating cheese for pasta. If it is not available, substitute Emmental.

Goat cheese (chèvre) can be fresh and mild or firm and pungent depending on its age and the way it is made. Some goat cheese is plain, while others are rolled in herbs, nuts, or spices such as black pepper or paprika. For the recipes in this book, a mild fresh goat cheese is all you need.

Parmigiano-Reggiano is an Italian cheese that is often used in French kitchens. For the best flavor, buy it in a chunk and grate it as needed, since it begins to dry out and lose flavor once it is grated.

CORNICHONS

Order some pâté, rillettes, ham, or sausages in France, and chances are, you will also be served a rustic crock full of crunchy cornichons: tart, tasty, bite-size pickles. The word *cornichon* means gherkin, a variety of tiny cucumber that is pickled with vinegar, spices, and pearl onions. Cornichons are widely available, but a dill pickle can be substituted if necessary.

CRÈME FRAÎCHE

Lightly soured and slightly nutty-tasting, crème fraîche is thicker than regular sour cream and not as tart. Crème fraîche does not curdle when heated, so it is often used in cooked sauces. It is not difficult to find in stores, but if you would like to make it yourself, it's easy to do (see box).

HOMEMADE CRÈME FRAÎCHE

This method works much better with cream that has not been ultrapasteurized. Warm 1 cup heavy cream just slightly and stir in 1 tablespoon buttermilk. Put the mixture in a covered jar and leave it in a warm place to thicken, 12 to 24 hours. Don't worry: the good bacteria in the buttermilk prevent the cream from spoiling. Once it has thickened, the crème fraîche can be stored in the refrigerator for up to 3 days.

DRIED BEANS

Many of the varieties of beans French cooks use are not common in the United States, but navy beans, pea beans, cannellini, or other small white beans are fine substitutes.

Flageolet beans are a French variety often served with lamb stew or roast lamb. Long and narrow with a lovely pale green color, these beans can be found at many specialty food stores. If you need to, you can substitute any small white bean.

Before slow cooking, dried beans must be soaked in cold water to cover by 2 inches for several hours or overnight. Or use the quick-soak method (see box).

TO QUICK-SOAK DRIED BEANS

Bring a saucepan of water to a boil. Add the beans, cover, and cook on low for 10 minutes. Let stand for 1 hour. Drain and rinse. Use as directed in the recipe.

DUCK FAT

Duck fat is used in many parts of France in place of butter or oil. Nutritionally similar to olive oil, it is used for making Duck Confit (page 72), frying potatoes, and many other preparations. Order duck fat online at dartagnan.com.

EXTRA-VIRGIN OLIVE OIL

Extra-virgin olive oil is not produced in large quantities in France, and exports are limited. If you can't find French olive oil, use extra-virgin olive oil from Liguria or Tuscany in Italy.

HERBS

Dried herbs are convenient, but when they are cooked in a slow cooker for a long time, their flavor can become overpowering. So when using dried herbs, I usually start out with a small amount. If the flavor of the dish needs perking up with more herbs, I add them at the end of the cooking time.

The flavor of fresh herbs, on the other hand, can sometimes disappear over the long cooking time. I often add some at the beginning, then stir in some more at the end of the cooking time.

Herbes de Provence is a commercial blend of dried herbs from the South of France that you can buy just about anywhere. Every manufacturer makes it a little differently, but typical ingredients include dried thyme, rosemary, savory, sage, basil, fennel seeds, and lavender. Use herbes de Provence in marinades and sauces.

JUNIPER BERRIES

Juniper berries are actually the tiny seed cones of juniper pines. They are used to flavor gin and as a seasoning for game, sauerkraut, and stews. Most stores with a good spice section have juniper berries, or you can order them online at williams-sonoma.com.

MUSTARD

No French kitchen would be without Dijon mustard. Golden brown and full-flavored, Dijon goes with sandwiches and charcuterie, is blended into sauces and dressings, and is used in marinades. It gets its name from the city of Dijon, in the Burgundy region of France, which was once a center of mustard production. Many flavored mustards are available, but for these recipes, you need only two kinds: smooth and coarse, with visible grains of mustard seeds.

OLIVES

Olives are often used in French cooking, especially the small purplish-brown niçoise variety. Cured in brine, niçoise olives are full-flavored but not overwhelming. If they are not available, substitute gaeta or kalamata olives.

ONION FAMILY

Leeks resemble oversized green onions or scallions. When buying leeks, look for fresh-looking root ends and green tops. Unlike scallions, leeks need cooking to tenderize them. They also need thorough cleaning, since soil is often trapped between the layers.

Shallots look like long, somewhat oval onions with papery brown skin and purplish flesh. They grow in clusters that vary in size. The flavor of shallots is said to be a cross between onions and garlic, but I find it is milder and mellower than either one. Shallots can be used raw or lightly cooked in vinaigrettes or sauces, they can be roasted or glazed and eaten whole, or they can be added to soups or stews for long, slow cooking.

PEPPER

A bright red pepper from the Basque region of France, piment d'Espelette, the Espelette pepper, is dried and used in all kinds of dishes. The flavor is sweet, mildly hot, and a bit smoky. It resembles a fine-quality paprika or cayenne, either of which can be substituted. Use it for eggs, sauces, and stews. Piment d'Espelette is available online at zingermans.com and in stores that carry a wide variety of spices.

SPELT

Spelt, an ancient grain similar to wheat, has recently become popular in French kitchens. It is used in soups and salads and cooked risotto-style. It has a nice nutty flavor and chewy texture. Barley, farro, or wheat berries can be substituted.

TOMATOES AND TOMATO PRODUCTS

Ripe tomatoes have a short season, but when they are available, I use them both raw and cooked. If I have the time, I like to remove the seeds and skins from fresh tomatoes before cooking with them (see box).

TO PEEL TOMATOES

Bring a pan of water deep enough to submerge the tomato to a boil and drop it in. When the water returns to the boil, count to 30, then remove the tomato with a slotted spoon. Place the tomato in ice water to cool, then cut it in half through the core. Cut away the core. The skin should slip right off in your hand. Squeeze the tomato to eliminate most of the seeds and the excess juice. Chop it and use in sauces or soup.

When good fresh tomatoes are not available, I cook with canned whole tomatoes, tomato puree, and tomato paste. For canned whole tomatoes, I like the long plum or pear-shaped tomatoes best. When I see a new brand, I buy just one can. At home, I open it to see whether the tomatoes are red from one end to the other and tender when cut. Greenish or white color on the ends indicates that the tomatoes were not ripe enough when they were picked, so they won't be very sweet. Hard tomatoes never cook down into a sauce. Two brands with tender tomatoes and a good tomato flavor are Coluccio and La Squisita.

Tomato puree is good for sauces when you want a smooth, thick texture. The puree should have a balanced tomato flavor, neither too sweet nor too acidic.

Tomato paste in tubes is a great convenience, since you don't have to open a whole can when you need just a spoonful or two to add color and flavor. Amore Tomato Paste is double concentrated for a deep tomato flavor and is widely available.

TRUFFLES

Truffles are fungi that grow under the ground like potatoes. Because they are somewhat rare, they can be very expensive. Truffle butter, made by blending chopped black or white truffles with butter, is a good way to add the unique flavor of truffles to eggs, chicken, potatoes, fish, and sauces. While the butter is not inexpensive, a little goes a long way. You can usually find truffle butter in specialty food stores, or you can order it online at amazon.com.

WINE

French cooks often use wine. Look for a red or white, according to the recipe, that is not too sweet or assertive so that it won't interfere with the other flavors in the dish. Don't hesitate to substitute another liquid such as broth, juice, beer, cider, or water, if you prefer.

Soups

Soups

Garlic Soup...23

Butternut Bisque 25

Tomato-Fennel Soup 26

Creamy Zucchini Soup...27

Soupe au Pistou (Provençal Vegetable Soup with Pesto) 28

Two-Way Potato-Leek Soup 30

Hot or Cold Carrot Soup with Tarragon Whipped Cream.....................31

Cauliflower Soup with Caviar 32

Parisian Split Pea Soup with Bacon and Croutons 33

Spinach and Egg Bouillabaisse 34

Bourride (Creamy Fish Soup) 36

Alsatian Lentil Soup with Bratwurst 38

Garbure (Cabbage and Bean Soup) 39

Chicken Broth 40

Classic French Beef Broth..41

Garlic Soup

Feel a cold coming on? This soup will cure you! It's an easy, creamy soup with the flavor of garlic mellowed by the long, slow cooking. It also makes a great first course or light supper.

When buying garlic, look for firm, plump heads with tight-fitting skins. Very dry, papery skins, green sprouts, or shriveled yellowish or brownish cloves are an indication that the garlic is past its prime.

SERVES 6

- 1 garlic head, cloves separated and peeled (about 20 cloves)
- 8 cups water
- 3 2-inch strips orange zest
- 2 bay leaves
- 6 fresh sage leaves
- 4 fresh thyme sprigs
- 2 teaspoons salt
- 3 large egg yolks
- ¼ cup extra-virgin olive oil
- 6 slices French bread, toasted
- 1 cup grated Emmental or Parmigiano-Reggiano cheese

In a large slow cooker, combine the garlic, water, orange zest, herbs, and salt.

Cover and cook on low for 6 hours.

Strain the soup through a sieve, pressing down on the solids and pushing the soft garlic through. In a large bowl, whisk the egg yolks and olive oil until thick. Gradually beat the hot soup into the egg mixture. Taste for seasoning.

Place a slice of toast in each bowl. Spoon in the soup, add a sprinkling of the cheese, and serve immediately.

Butternut Bisque

The sunny color and mild, sweet flavor of this soup make it very appealing. Serve it as a first course before a roast chicken, or pour it into mugs to enjoy with a ham sandwich.

SERVES 6 TO 8

- 1 large butternut squash (about 2 pounds), peeled, seeded, and cut into 1-inch pieces
- 1 medium onion, chopped
- 1 large sweet apple, such as Fuji or Golden Delicious, peeled, cored, and chopped
- 6 cups Chicken Broth (page 40), store-bought chicken broth, vegetable broth, or water
- Salt
- ½ cup heavy cream, plus more for garnish
- Pinch of freshly grated nutmeg, plus more for garnish
- Sliced apples, for garnish

In a large slow cooker, combine the squash, onion, apple, and broth. Add 1 teaspoon salt.

Cover and cook on low for 6 hours, or until the vegetables are very soft. Let cool slightly. Transfer the soup to a blender and puree until smooth. Add the cream and nutmeg and blend again. Reheat if necessary. Taste for seasoning and add more salt if needed.

Spoon the soup into serving bowls, drizzle each serving with a teaspoon of heavy cream, garnish with the nutmeg and apple slices, and serve hot.

Tomato-Fennel Soup

Fennel adds an intriguing flavor to this light tomato soup. Serve it with open-faced toasted cheese sandwiches or, better yet, a *croque-monsieur*, a French-style grilled ham-and-cheese sandwich.

SERVES 8

- 2 medium fennel bulbs (about 2 pounds)
- 2 medium onions, sliced
- 2 medium boiling potatoes, such as Yukon Gold, peeled and chopped
- 4 tomatoes, peeled, seeded, and chopped, or one 28-ounce can tomatoes with their juice
- 6 cups Chicken Broth (page 40), store-bought chicken broth, vegetable broth, or water
- Salt and freshly ground pepper
- Extra-virgin olive oil

Trim the fennel and set aside some of the green fronds for garnish. Chop the fennel into 1-inch pieces.

Combine the vegetables and broth in a large slow cooker. Add salt and pepper to taste. Cover and cook on low for 6 hours, or until the vegetables are very soft.

Let cool slightly. Pass the soup through a food mill set over a bowl or transfer to a blender and puree. Reheat if necessary. Taste for seasoning.

Pour the soup into bowls. Drizzle with a little olive oil, sprinkle with some of the fennel fronds, and serve hot.

Creamy Zucchini Soup

Although this soup is creamy and rich, it has no cream at all. The secret is the rice, which thickens the soup and gives it a smooth texture. A little freshly grated Parmesan adds richness, while fresh parsley perks up the flavor.

SERVES 6 TO 8

- 2 tablespoons olive oil
- 2 large onions, chopped
- 1 garlic clove, chopped
- 2 fresh sage leaves
- 1½ pounds zucchini, trimmed and thickly sliced
- 6 cups water
- Salt and freshly ground pepper
- ¼ cup long-grain white rice
- ½ cup freshly grated Parmigiano-Reggiano
- ¼ cup chopped fresh flat-leaf parsley

In a large skillet, heat the oil over medium heat. Add the onions and cook, stirring frequently, until golden, about 10 minutes. Stir in the garlic and sage.

Scrape the onion mixture into a large slow cooker. Add the zucchini, water, and salt and pepper to taste. Cover and cook on high for 3 hours. Add the rice and cook for 30 minutes more, or until the rice is very tender.

Transfer the soup to a blender and puree until smooth. Reheat if necessary. Taste for seasoning. Serve hot, sprinkled with the cheese and parsley.

Soupe au Pistou
(Provençal Vegetable Soup with Pesto)

Since the Provence region of France adjoins Italy, it's no surprise that many of the dishes on both sides of the border have similar flavors. This vegetable soup, fragrant with garlic and basil pesto, is a perfect example. I make it year-round, varying the vegetables according to the season. Try it with green beans, fresh fava beans, or lima beans—whatever looks best.

SERVES 8

4	medium carrots, peeled and chopped
3	medium boiling potatoes, such as Yukon Gold, peeled and chopped
2	medium onions, chopped
1½	cups chopped canned tomatoes
2	medium zucchini, chopped
8	cups water
	Salt and freshly ground pepper
2	cups cooked or drained canned cannellini beans
1	cup small pasta, such as ditalini or elbows
	Pesto (page 219)

In a large slow cooker, combine the carrots, potatoes, onions, tomatoes, zucchini, and water. Season with salt and pepper to taste.

Cover and cook on low for 8 hours, or until the vegetables are tender. Stir in the beans and pasta. Cook until the pasta is tender, about 30 minutes. Taste for seasoning.

Spoon the soup into serving bowls. Top each bowl with a spoonful of the pesto and serve hot.

Two-Way Potato-Leek Soup

This potato and leek soup is a cook's dream, since there are so many ways to vary it. I call it two-way because I like to serve it either hot or cold, but you have several different options for changing it (see Variations).

SERVES 6

- 2 medium onions, sliced
- 2 medium leeks, trimmed, well washed, and sliced
- 4 medium boiling potatoes, such as Yukon Gold, peeled and sliced
- 4 cups Chicken Broth (page 40), store-bought chicken broth, vegetable broth, or water
- 4 cups water
- Salt and freshly ground pepper
- ½ cup heavy cream

In a large slow cooker, combine the onions, leeks, potatoes, broth, and water. Add salt and pepper to taste. Cover and cook on low for 8 hours, or until the vegetables are tender. Let cool slightly. Transfer the soup to a blender and puree until smooth.

If you are serving the soup hot, reheat if necessary. Stir in the cream and taste for seasoning. Serve hot or chill completely and serve cold.

Variations

Serve hot or cold with chopped chives and a drizzle of crème fraîche or heavy cream.

Serve hot or cold with a handful of chopped watercress stirred in.

Serve hot topped with crumbled crisp bacon.

Serve hot topped with crumbled mild blue cheese, such as Bleu d'Auvergne or Maytag Blue.

Serve hot with a spoonful of Pesto (page 219).

Hot or Cold Carrot Soup with Tarragon Whipped Cream

Don't put your slow cooker away when the weather turns warm! Make delicious cold soups like this one, and serve with a green salad for a light summer meal. The soup tastes great hot too, topped with Herb Croutons (page 216).

SERVES 6

- 2 tablespoons unsalted butter
- 4 large shallots, chopped (about 1 cup)
- 3 pounds carrots, peeled and coarsely chopped
- 4 cups Chicken Broth (page 40), store-bought chicken broth, vegetable broth, or water
- 4 cups water

  Salt and freshly ground pepper
- ½ cup heavy cream, well chilled
- 1 tablespoon minced fresh tarragon, dill, or basil

In a medium skillet, melt the butter over medium heat. Add the shallots and cook, stirring often, until they are very tender and golden, about 5 minutes.

Place the carrots in a large slow cooker. Add the shallots, broth, water, and salt and pepper to taste. Cover and cook on high for 6 hours, or until the carrots are tender.

Let cool slightly. Transfer to a blender and puree until smooth. To serve hot, reheat the soup if necessary. To serve cold, chill for several hours or overnight.

Just before serving, taste for seasoning. In a chilled bowl with chilled beaters, whip the cream until light. Fold in the herbs.

Spoon the soup into bowls, top each with a dollop of the herbed cream, and serve.

Cauliflower Soup with Caviar

The optional caviar garnish adds a sophisticated and colorful touch to this creamy soup. Use an inexpensive variety, such as whitefish or salmon caviar.

SERVES 6

- 1 large cauliflower (about 2½ pounds)
- 1 medium onion, chopped
- 4 cups Chicken Broth (page 40), store-bought chicken broth, vegetable broth, or water
- Salt and freshly ground pepper
- ½ cup heavy cream
- Caviar and minced fresh chives (optional)

Cut the cauliflower into 1-inch pieces and discard the tough stems. Place the cauliflower in a large slow cooker. Add the onion, broth, and salt and pepper to taste. If necessary, add a little water to just cover the cauliflower.

Cover and cook on low for 5 hours, or until the cauliflower is very soft. Transfer to a blender and puree until smooth. Add the heavy cream and blend again. Reheat if necessary. Taste for seasoning and serve hot, garnished with the caviar and chives, if using.

Parisian Split Pea Soup
with Bacon and Croutons

A frosty mist swirled through the streets of Paris one January day as my husband and I made our way toward a little bistro. When the waiter brought steaming bowls of the *soupe du jour* to the next table, I ordered the same thing: this thick, aromatic soup, fragrant with herbs and smoky bacon. It was just the thing! Serve it with "Roasted" Beet Salad with Roquefort and Walnuts (page 154).

SERVES 6 TO 8

- 1   pound split peas
- 4   ounces bacon
- 1   small onion, chopped
- 1   large carrot, peeled and chopped
- 1   celery rib, chopped
- 2   tablespoons chopped fresh flat-leaf parsley
- ½   teaspoon chopped fresh thyme
- 1   bay leaf
- 8   cups Chicken Broth (page 40), store-bought chicken broth, or water
      Salt and freshly ground pepper
      Croutons (page 216)

Rinse the split peas and drain them in a colander. Discard any shriveled peas.

In a large skillet, cook the bacon, turning, until crisp on both sides. Remove the bacon, but leave the fat in the pan. Drain the bacon on paper towels. Crumble the bacon and set it aside to garnish the soup.

Add the onion, carrot, and celery to the skillet with the bacon fat and cook, stirring often, until softened and golden, about 10 minutes. Scrape the vegetables into a large slow cooker. Add the split peas, herbs, broth, and salt and pepper to taste.

Cover and cook on low for 8 hours, or until the peas are tender. Cool slightly. Discard the bay leaf. Transfer to a blender, puree until smooth, and reheat if necessary.

Taste for seasoning and serve hot, sprinkled with the bacon and croutons.

Spinach and Egg Bouillabaisse

When I first visited Provence, I was surprised to learn that bouillabaisse, which I always thought of as a fish soup, can also be made with vegetables and chicken. Then I discovered this sensational meatless version. Each portion is served with a poached egg on top. When your spoon touches the softly cooked egg, the yolk oozes into the soup.

Poaching the eggs on the soup may seem tricky, but it is really quite easy. Just be sure to break the eggs, one at a time, into a cup first, and then carefully slip each egg onto the surface of the soup. If an egg breaks before you serve it, don't be concerned. The soup will still taste great.

SERVES 6

6 russet (baking) potatoes, peeled and chopped

1 large onion, chopped

3 cups Chicken Broth (page 40), store-bought chicken broth, vegetable broth, or water

3 cups water

Salt and freshly ground pepper

1 10-ounce package frozen chopped spinach, thawed

6 large eggs

1 baguette, cut into ½-inch-thick slices and toasted

Freshly grated Parmigiano-Reggiano, Aioli (page 217), or Rouille (page 218)

In a large slow cooker, combine the potatoes, onion, chicken broth, and water. Season with salt and pepper to taste. Cover and cook on high for 6 hours, or until the potatoes are very tender. Stir in the spinach and cook for 15 minutes, or until the spinach is hot.

When ready to serve, break 1 egg into a small cup. Remove the cover of the slow cooker and, holding the cup close to the surface, pour in the egg. Repeat with the remaining 5 eggs, placing them about an inch apart on the soup. Cover and cook for 5 minutes, or until the eggs are done to taste.

Place a slice or two of toast in each soup bowl. Carefully spoon an egg and some of the soup over the toast. Sprinkle with the cheese or pass the aioli or rouille. Serve hot.

Bourride (Creamy Fish Soup)

Rich and creamy, this soup can be a one-pot meal. Monkfish is typically used in this dish in France, but any firm-fleshed fish or shellfish can be substituted. Sea scallops are a good choice because of their firm texture and sweet flavor.

SERVES 6

- 1 pound boiling potatoes, such as Yukon Gold, peeled and chopped
- 1 leek, trimmed, well washed, and thinly sliced
- 2 medium carrots, peeled and chopped
- 1 small fennel bulb, trimmed and chopped
- 1 garlic clove, minced
- 2 3-inch strips orange zest
- 1 bay leaf
- 6 cups water
- 1 cup dry white wine
- Salt and freshly ground pepper
- 1½ pounds monkfish or sea scallops
- 1 cup Aioli (page 217)
- ¼ cup heavy cream or crème fraîche (see page 14)
- Chopped chives
- Croutons (page 216)

In a large slow cooker, combine the potatoes, leek, carrots, fennel, garlic, orange zest, and bay leaf. Add the water, wine, and salt and pepper to taste. Cover and cook on low for 8 hours, or until the vegetables are tender.

With a sharp knife, remove the connective tissue from the monkfish. Cut the fish into bite-size pieces. If using scallops, cut them into halves or quarters depending on their size. Add the seafood to the soup. Cover and cook for 5 minutes more, or until just cooked through.

In a large bowl, whisk together the aioli and cream. Add 1 cup of the hot broth to the bowl and whisk until blended. Pour the broth-cream mixture into the soup and stir to combine. Discard the bay leaf. Taste for seasoning.

Spoon the soup into bowls and sprinkle each with chives. Serve hot with croutons.

Alsatian Lentil Soup with Bratwurst

Because Alsace shares a long border with Germany, the foods of the two regions have similar flavors and ingredients. This rich soup is a perfect example. Serve it with rye bread and French Muenster cheese for a hearty dinner.

SERVES 8

- 1 pound brown lentils, rinsed and picked over
- 4 bratwursts
- 4 celery ribs, chopped
- 2 medium carrots, peeled and chopped
- 2 medium leeks, trimmed, well washed, and chopped
- 1 bay leaf
- ½ teaspoon chopped fresh thyme
- Salt and freshly ground pepper to taste
- 8 cups water
- Crème fraîche (see page 14) or sour cream

In a large slow cooker, combine all the ingredients except for the crème fraîche. Cover and cook on low for 6 to 8 hours, or until the lentils are tender.

Discard the bay leaf. Remove the bratwurst and cut it into slices. Stir the slices into the soup. Taste for seasoning.

Serve the soup hot, topping each bowl with a dollop of crème fraîche.

Garbure (Cabbage and Bean Soup)

Popular in several regions of southwestern France, garbure is a vegetable soup or stew—how thick depends on how much liquid you add to the pot. Some French cooks say it should be thick enough that a spoon can stand upright in it.

Everyone makes garbure his or her own way, and since it is eaten year-round, the vegetables vary with the season. As for the meats, some cooks use duck or goose confit, while others use pork, ham, and sausage. The only ingredients that seem to remain constant are the white beans and cabbage. Napa and savoy cabbages are milder than regular green cabbage.

SERVES 8

1 pound white beans, such as navy or cannellini beans

1¼ pounds smoked ham hocks

4 medium carrots, peeled and chopped

3 medium boiling potatoes, such as Yukon Gold, peeled and chopped

5 cups shredded napa or savoy cabbage (about half of a large head)

4 garlic cloves, minced

1 large onion, chopped

1 teaspoon chopped fresh thyme

1 bay leaf

8 cups water

Salt and freshly ground pepper

Soak the beans in cold water to cover overnight or quick-soak them (see page 16). Drain well.

Place the beans in a large slow cooker. Add the ham hocks, carrots, potatoes, cabbage, garlic, onion, herbs, water, and salt and pepper to taste. Cover and cook on low for 8 to 10 hours, or until the beans and the meat are tender.

Remove the ham hocks and cut the meat into ½-inch pieces. Stir the meat into the soup. Taste for seasoning. Discard the bay leaf and serve hot.

Chicken Broth

This French-style chicken broth is easy and economical, especially if you use trimmings like wing tips and backs and the giblets found inside whole birds. Do not use the livers, however, since their flavor is too strong. Turkey parts, if you have some, are good too, and add extra flavor.

MAKES ABOUT 2½ QUARTS

- 3 pounds chicken wings, backs, giblets, or other parts
- 3 medium carrots, coarsely chopped
- 1 large onion, stuck with a clove
- 2 celery ribs, coarsely chopped
- 1 leek, trimmed, well washed, and coarsely chopped
- 2 fresh flat-leaf parsley sprigs
- 1 garlic clove, peeled
- 1 bay leaf
- 1 teaspoon whole peppercorns
- 10 cups water

Combine all the ingredients in a large slow cooker. Cover and cook on low for 8 to 10 hours.

Let cool slightly. Strain the broth into a bowl and discard the solids. Refrigerate until cold. Remove the fat from the surface.

Use within 3 days or freeze in small containers for up to 6 months.

Classic French Beef Broth

Save scraps of beef and bones in a plastic bag in the freezer until you have enough to make this hearty and inexpensive broth. Browning the scraps in the oven before slow cooking them adds color and enriches the flavor.

MAKES ABOUT 2½ QUARTS

- 2 pounds beef bones
- 1 pound beef trimmings or an inexpensive cut, such as beef chuck
- 3 large onions, quartered
- 2 large carrots, quartered
- 10 cups water
- 3 celery ribs, coarsely chopped
- 1 medium tomato, chopped
- 2 garlic cloves, peeled
  A few fresh flat-leaf parsley sprigs
- 1 fresh thyme sprig
- 1 bay leaf
- 6 whole peppercorns
  Salt to taste

Preheat the oven to 450°F. Spread the bones and trimmings in a large roasting pan. Add the onions and carrots. Place the pan in the oven and roast for 45 minutes, or until nicely browned.

Transfer the browned bones, meat, and vegetables to a large slow cooker. Pour off any fat in the roasting pan. Add 1 cup of the water to the pan and cook over medium heat, scraping the bottom of the pan to loosen any browned bits.

Pour the liquid into the slow cooker. Add the remaining 9 cups water and the remaining ingredients.

Cover and cook on low for 10 to 12 hours. Let cool slightly. Strain the broth into a bowl and discard the solids. Refrigerate until cold. Remove the fat from the surface.

Use within 3 days or freeze in small containers for up to 6 months.

Mustard Pommery
PRODUCT OF FRANCE

It was in the year 1760 that
a superior of the ancient
religious order of Meaux
transmitted to the
Pommery family
the secret recipe
of their marve-
lous speciality
"Moutarde des
Chanoines", the
Abbot's Mustard.
This mustard has been
served at the tables of
kings of France since

Chicken, Turkey, and Duck

Chicken, Turkey, and Duck

Sunday Roast Chicken with Potatoes, Lemon, and Thyme................45

Herbed Roast Chicken with Garlic and Shallots 47

Chicken Salad Parisienne...48

Chicken in Half Mourning 51

Chicken with Escargot Butter 52

Chicken in the Pot with Aioli 53

Chicken with Tarragon, Mustard, and Cream 54

Corsican Chicken with Sun-Dried Tomatoes 55

Basque Chicken with Ham and Sweet Peppers 56

Chicken Bouillabaisse 57

Chicken with Forty Cloves of Garlic 58

Moroccan Chicken with Apricots and Almonds 59

Chicken with Figs 60

Chicken Pan Bagnat (Niçoise Chicken Sandwich) 62

Silky Chicken Liver Mousse 64

Provençal Spinach Meatballs 67

Dijon-Style Cornish Hens with Mustard Sauce 69

Duxelles-Stuffed Turkey Breast 70

Duck Confit..72

Crispy Duck Confit 74

Sunday Roast Chicken with Potatoes, Lemon, and Thyme

A big, juicy chicken with potatoes cooked in the chicken juices is my idea of a great dinner any time. Add some vegetables like red onions, leeks, carrots, mushrooms, parsnips, rutabaga, or turnips, if you like.

SERVES 4

- 4 medium boiling potatoes, such as Yukon Gold, peeled and thickly sliced
- 2 garlic cloves, chopped, plus 4 whole garlic cloves, peeled
  Salt and freshly ground pepper
- 1 chicken (about 4 pounds)
- 3–4 fresh thyme sprigs or a pinch of herbes de provence
- 1 lemon, cut in half
- 1 tablespoon olive oil
- 1 tablespoon cornstarch, blended with 2 tablespoons cool water
- 1 tablespoon unsalted butter

Scatter the potatoes and chopped garlic in a large slow cooker and sprinkle with salt and pepper to taste.

Remove the neck and giblets from the chicken cavity and reserve them for another use. Trim away any excess fat.

Sprinkle the chicken inside and out with salt and pepper to taste. Put the whole garlic cloves, thyme, and lemon halves inside the cavity and place the chicken in the slow cooker. Rub it all over with the olive oil. Cover and cook on low for 6 hours, or until the chicken is tender and the temperature in the thickest part of the thigh measures 165°F on an instant-read thermometer.

Remove the chicken and potatoes from the slow cooker and cut the chicken into serving pieces, reserving the lemon halves. Cover and keep warm.

Skim the fat from the pan juices. Place the chicken juices in a small saucepan and bring them to a simmer. Squeeze the lemon halves (carefully; they're hot) into the juices. Add the cornstarch mixture and cook, stirring, until slightly thickened. Stir in the butter.

Drizzle the pan juices over the chicken. Serve hot with the potatoes.

Herbed Roast Chicken with Garlic and Shallots

A generous rubdown with typical Provençal herbs and seasonings makes for a great-tasting chicken. Serve it hot with mashed potatoes and a green vegetable or cold with a dab of mayonnaise and a tomato salad. The chicken is also good for Chicken Salad Parisienne (page 48) or Chicken Pan Bagnat (page 62).

SERVES 4

- 1 chicken (about 4 pounds)
- 2 tablespoons chopped fresh flat-leaf parsley
- 1 tablespoon chopped fresh rosemary
- ½ teaspoon fennel seeds, crushed
- 8 garlic cloves, peeled
- 1 teaspoon salt
  Freshly ground pepper
- 2 tablespoons olive oil
- 3 large shallots, sliced

Remove the neck and giblets from the chicken cavity and reserve them for another use. Trim away any excess fat.

Chop together the parsley, rosemary, fennel seeds, and 3 of the garlic cloves. Place the mixture in a small bowl and add the salt, a generous grind of pepper, and the oil. Place about one third of the mixture inside the chicken cavity along with the remaining 5 garlic cloves. Spread the rest of the herb mixture over the chicken. Place the chicken in a large slow cooker. Sprinkle with the shallots.

Cover and cook on low for 6 hours, or until the chicken is tender and the temperature in the thickest part of the thigh measures 165°F on an instant-read thermometer. Cut the chicken into serving pieces and serve with the cooking juices.

OUT OF THE POT *Chicken Salad Parisienne*

Served with French bread, a green salad, and chilled rosé, this salad makes a great summer lunch or supper.

SERVES 4 TO 6

         Herbed Roast Chicken with Garlic and Shallots (page 47)

6–12 **small waxy potatoes, such as Yukon Gold, cooked and sliced**

   8 **ounces green beans, cooked**

   2 **tablespoons capers, rinsed and drained**

       Vinaigrette (page 220)

       Lettuce leaves

   3 **hard-cooked eggs, peeled and quartered**

   1 **cup halved cherry or grape tomatoes**

Discard the chicken skin and bones and cut the meat into bite-size pieces. In a bowl, combine the chicken, potatoes, green beans, and capers. Drizzle with half of the dressing.

Arrange the lettuce leaves on a serving platter. Pile the chicken mixture on top. Garnish with the eggs and tomatoes. Drizzle with the remaining dressing and serve.

Chicken in Half Mourning

Despite the moniker, there is nothing gloomy about this flavorful chicken! The name comes from the traditional way of making it by sliding paper-thin slices of black truffles underneath the skin. The cook who came up with the idea must have been reminded of the somber black garb worn to a funeral.

Truffles are awfully expensive, but truffle butter, which has recently become widely available, is an affordable substitute. It is not inexpensive, but it does add a luxurious flavor at a relatively low cost. Serve this at your fanciest dinner parties.

The cooking juices and any leftover truffle butter can be tossed with pasta or rice or added to mashed potatoes.

SERVES 4

- 2 medium carrots, peeled and sliced
- 1 celery rib, sliced
- 1 leek, trimmed, well washed, and halved lengthwise
- 1 chicken (about 4 pounds)
  Salt and freshly ground pepper
- 2 tablespoons black truffle butter (see page 19)
- ½ cup heavy cream

Scatter the vegetables in the bottom of a large slow cooker.

Remove the neck and giblets from the chicken cavity and reserve them for another use. Trim away any excess fat.

Sprinkle the chicken inside and out with salt and pepper to taste. Carefully lift the skin covering the legs and breasts. With your fingers, spread the truffle butter on the meat, beneath the skin. Place the chicken in the slow cooker. Cover and cook on low for 6 hours, or until the chicken is tender and the temperature in the thickest part of the thigh measures 165°F on an instant-read thermometer.

Remove the chicken to a platter and cover to keep warm. Strain the pan juices into a small saucepan and skim off the excess fat. Bring the juices to a simmer. Add the cream and boil rapidly until slightly thickened. Taste for seasoning.

Carve the chicken and serve with the sauce.

Chicken with Escargot Butter

In my opinion, the best thing about the French classic *Escargots Bourguignons* is not the snails but, rather, the mouthwatering parsley and garlic butter that covers them. It's too good to be relegated to the occasional escargot. I like to slather the butter under the skin of a chicken before "roasting" it in the slow cooker.

SERVES 4

- 2 tablespoons unsalted butter, softened
- ½ cup finely chopped fresh flat-leaf parsley
- 2 tablespoons minced shallot or onion
- 1 garlic clove, finely chopped
- Salt and freshly ground pepper
- 1 chicken (about 4 pounds)

In a small bowl, mash the butter with the parsley, shallot, garlic, 1 teaspoon salt, and ½ teaspoon pepper.

Remove the neck and giblets from the chicken cavity and reserve them for another use. Trim away any excess fat.

Sprinkle the chicken inside and out with salt and pepper to taste. Carefully lift the skin covering the legs and breasts. With your fingers, spread the garlic butter on the meat, beneath the skin. Place a little of the mixture inside the chicken. Place the chicken in a large slow cooker. Cover and cook on low for 6 hours, or until the chicken is tender and the temperature in the thickest part of the thigh measures 165°F on an instant-read thermometer.

Remove the chicken from the slow cooker and cut it into serving pieces. Skim the fat from the pan juices. Drizzle the pan juices over the chicken and serve hot.

Chicken in the Pot with Aioli

Henri IV, who was the king of France from 1589 to 1610, is credited with the phrase "a chicken in every pot," meant to signify a minimum level of prosperity for every *citoyen*. Even today, chicken in the pot is a favorite French Sunday dinner. Serve it with a garlicky aioli and cornichons.

SERVES 4

- 6 garlic cloves, peeled
- 2 large carrots, peeled and quartered
- 2 celery ribs, quartered
- 2 small leeks, trimmed, well washed, and halved lengthwise
- 4 baby turnips, trimmed, or 1 large turnip, peeled and quartered
- 1 small onion, chopped
- 1 3-inch sprig fresh rosemary
  Salt and freshly ground pepper
- 1 chicken (about 4 pounds)
- 1 cup Chicken Broth (page 40) or store-bought chicken broth
  Aioli (page 217)
  Cornichons

Scatter the vegetables and rosemary in a large slow cooker. Sprinkle with salt and pepper to taste.

Remove the neck and giblets from the chicken cavity and reserve them for another use. Trim away any excess fat. Sprinkle the chicken inside and out with salt and pepper to taste. Place the chicken on top of the vegetables and add the broth. Cover and cook on low for 6 hours, or until the chicken is tender and the temperature in the thickest part of the thigh measures 165°F on an instant-read thermometer.

Carve the chicken and serve it in shallow bowls with the vegetables and cooking liquid. Pass the aioli and cornichons.

Chicken with Tarragon, Mustard, and Cream

The first time this dish was put in front of me, I remember thinking, if only it tastes as good as it smells. To my surprise, it was even better! Meaty chicken thighs are slathered with Dijon mustard, then sprinkled with tarragon, parsley, and garlic. For very little effort, the slow-cooked thighs come out tender and moist, while the pan juices are transformed into a flavorful and creamy sauce. Serve with rice or noodles and a green vegetable such as asparagus or tiny peas.

SERVES 4 TO 6

- ½ cup chicken broth
- 2 tablespoons red wine vinegar
- 3 tablespoons Dijon mustard
- Salt and freshly ground pepper
- 8–12 bone-in chicken thighs, skin removed
- 2 garlic cloves, finely chopped
- 3 tablespoons chopped fresh flat-leaf parsley, plus more for garnish
- 1 teaspoon chopped fresh tarragon, plus more for garnish
- ⅓ cup heavy cream

Pour the broth and vinegar into a large slow cooker.

Stir the mustard together with salt and pepper to taste. Brush the chicken all over with the seasoned mustard. Arrange the chicken pieces in the slow cooker, overlapping them slightly. Sprinkle with the garlic, parsley, and tarragon.

Cover and cook on low for 5 hours, or until the chicken is tender and cooked through.

Remove the chicken to a serving plate and cover to keep warm. Strain the pan juices into a saucepan and skim off the excess fat. Bring the juices to a simmer over high heat. Stir in the cream and return to a simmer. Taste for seasoning. Pour the sauce over the chicken. Sprinkle with the chopped fresh herbs and serve hot.

Corsican Chicken with Sun-Dried Tomatoes

The island of Corsica has been invaded by many different armies and has been passed back and forth between Italy and France. Although it became a part of France in the eighteenth century, the food, like this rustic chicken dish, still shows a strong Italian influence.

SERVES 6

- 4 pounds bone-in chicken legs, thighs, and breasts
- 2 garlic cloves, chopped
- Salt and freshly ground pepper
- ½ cup chopped oil-packed sun-dried tomatoes
- ½ cup thinly cut strips roasted red bell pepper
- 1 tablespoon chopped fresh rosemary
- ½ cup chicken broth
- 1 tablespoon cornstarch, blended with 2 tablespoons cool water
- ¼ cup chopped fresh basil

Remove the skin from the chicken thighs and legs. Place the chicken in a large slow cooker and sprinkle it with the garlic. Season with salt and pepper to taste. Add the tomatoes with a little of their oil, the peppers, rosemary, and broth. Cover and cook on low for 5 hours, or until the chicken is tender and cooked through.

With a slotted spoon, remove the chicken and vegetables to a platter and cover to keep warm. Pour the remaining liquid into a small saucepan and spoon off the fat from the surface. Bring the juices to a boil over high heat. Stir the cornstarch mixture into the juices. Cook, stirring, until slightly thickened. Taste for seasoning.

Stir in the basil and pour the sauce over the chicken. Serve hot.

Basque Chicken with Ham and Sweet Peppers

Espelette pepper (piment d'Espelette) is the signature seasoning of Basque cooking. If you visit this area of France during the harvest, you will see handmade strings of the bright red peppers hanging from doorways and racks to dry in the open air. Once dried, the peppers are crushed or ground and used to brighten just about everything, from fried eggs to meat and fish. The flavor is sweet and smoky, similar to a medium-hot paprika or chili powder. Together with bell peppers, tomato, and smoked ham, piment adds character to this saucy chicken.

SERVES 4

- 2 tablespoons olive oil
- 2 medium onions, chopped
- 4 garlic cloves, finely chopped
- 4 ounces smoked ham, cut into small dice
- 1 28-ounce can tomato puree
- 3 red or yellow bell peppers, cut into bite-size pieces
- 1 teaspoon piment d'Espelette (see page 18), paprika, or chili powder
- 1 bay leaf
- ½ teaspoon dried thyme
  Salt
- 4 pounds bone-in chicken legs, thighs, and breasts

In a large skillet, heat the oil over medium heat. Add the onions and garlic and cook, stirring often, until the onions are golden, about 10 minutes. Stir in the ham and cook for 5 minutes more. Scrape the mixture into a large slow cooker.

Add the tomato puree, bell peppers, piment d'Espelette, bay leaf, thyme, and salt to taste. Stir well. Remove the skin from the chicken thighs and legs. Add the chicken pieces, pressing them into the sauce. Cover and cook on low for 5 to 6 hours, or until the chicken is tender and cooked through. Discard the bay leaf and serve hot.

Chicken Bouillabaisse

In this version of that Provençal specialty, bouillabaisse, chicken is the star, simmering in a deeply satisfying garlicky broth. And, just like the classic seafood bouillabaisse, the chicken is served in bowls with toasted French bread and rouille.

SERVES 4 TO 8

- 2 tablespoons olive oil
- 2 large onions, chopped
- 2 garlic cloves, chopped
- 1 cup dry white wine
- 1 cup chopped canned or fresh tomatoes
- ½ cup tomato puree
- 2 3-inch strips orange zest
- Big pinch of saffron threads, crumbled
- ½ teaspoon fennel seeds
- Pinch of piment d'Espelette (see page 18) or cayenne
- 8 bone-in chicken thighs, skin removed
- Salt and freshly ground pepper
- 8 ½-inch-thick slices French or Italian bread, toasted
- Rouille (page 218)

In a large skillet, heat the oil over medium heat. Add the onions and garlic and cook until tender and golden, about 8 minutes. Add the wine and bring to a simmer. Pour the mixture into a large slow cooker. Stir in the tomatoes, tomato puree, orange zest, saffron, fennel seeds, and piment d'Espelette.

Sprinkle the chicken with salt and pepper to taste. Place the pieces in the slow cooker, spooning some of the sauce over the top. Cover and cook on low for 6 hours, or until the chicken is tender and coming away from the bone.

Serve the chicken and sauce in shallow bowls with the toast and rouille.

Chicken with Forty Cloves of Garlic

Don't be alarmed by the quantity of garlic in this recipe! The long, slow cooking in this French bistro classic turns it mellow, nutty-tasting, and soft, just like roasted garlic. Mash some of the cloves into the pan juices before serving, and spoon the remaining garlic over the chicken. Provide plenty of French bread to eat with it.

SERVES 6

2–3 garlic heads
12 bone-in chicken thighs, skin removed
1 tablespoon chopped fresh rosemary
Salt and freshly ground pepper
½ cup dry white wine
2 tablespoons fresh lemon juice

Separate the garlic into cloves. There should be about 40. Discard any loose skin from the garlic cloves, but do not peel them. Scatter the garlic in a large slow cooker.

Sprinkle the chicken with the rosemary and salt and pepper to taste. Place the chicken pieces in the slow cooker. Pour in the wine and lemon juice. Cover and cook on low for 5 to 6 hours, or until the chicken is tender and cooked through.

To serve, transfer the chicken and most of the garlic to a large platter. Cover and keep warm. Remove and smash the remaining garlic cloves and stir them back into the liquid. Discard the skins.

Pour the liquid into a saucepan and bring it to a boil. Cook until reduced and slightly thickened. Taste for seasoning. Pour the sauce over the chicken and serve hot.

Moroccan Chicken with Apricots and Almonds

Couscous, either whole grain or regular, is the perfect accompaniment to this lightly spiced chicken.

SERVES 8

- 2 tablespoons olive oil
- 2 large onions, chopped
- 2 garlic cloves, finely chopped
- 2 tablespoons all-purpose flour
- 2 teaspoons paprika
- 1 teaspoon ground ginger
- 1 teaspoon ground cumin
- 2 cups Chicken Broth (page 40) or store-bought chicken broth
- 2 tablespoons fresh lemon juice
- 2 tablespoons honey
- 1 cup dried apricot halves, quartered
- 8 skinless, boneless chicken breast halves
  Salt and freshly ground pepper
- 2 tablespoons sliced toasted almonds
  Chopped fresh cilantro

In a large skillet, heat the oil over medium heat. Add the onions and garlic and cook, stirring frequently, until the onions are golden, about 10 minutes. Mix in the flour and spices and cook for 1 minute. Whisk in the broth, lemon juice, and honey. Bring to a simmer and cook until slightly thickened, about 5 minutes. Stir in the apricots.

Pour half of the sauce into a large slow cooker. Sprinkle the chicken with salt and pepper to taste. Place the chicken in the cooker, overlapping the pieces slightly. Drizzle with the remaining sauce. Cover and cook on low for 2½ to 3 hours, or until the chicken is cooked through.

Serve the chicken sprinkled with the almonds and cilantro.

Chicken with Figs

Sweet figs have a short season during the summer months, when they are best eaten fresh with salty ham or a dab of goat cheese or baked into desserts. When fresh figs are not available, most markets sell them dried in the same department as the raisins and prunes. The most common dried fig varieties are the dark brown Mission and light brown Calimyrna. They are good with a cheese platter, accompanied by toasted nuts, or poached in liquid to go with ice cream or yogurt.

At a bistro in Paris, my husband had duck cooked with figs, and we have been crazy about the combination ever since. I decided to try the same thing with chicken thighs, since this part of the bird is tender and rich like duck, but much more available. The results are sensational.

SERVES 6

- 12   bone-in chicken thighs, skin removed
  -     Salt and freshly ground pepper
- 3   medium shallots, sliced
- 2   bay leaves
- 4   fresh thyme sprigs
- ½   cup dry white wine or chicken broth
- 2   tablespoons sherry vinegar
- 1   tablespoon honey
- 12   dried Black Mission figs

Sprinkle the chicken all over with salt and pepper to taste. Scatter half of the shallots in a large slow cooker. Place the chicken in the cooker. Tuck the bay leaves between the chicken pieces. Scatter the remaining shallots and the thyme over all.

Stir together the wine, vinegar, and honey and pour the mixture over the chicken. Cover and cook on low for 5 hours, or until the chicken is tender and cooked through.

While the chicken is cooking, place the figs in hot water to cover for at least 30 minutes. Drain the figs.

Remove the chicken pieces to a serving platter and cover to keep warm. Discard the bay leaves. Pour the cooking juices into a small skillet and add the figs. Bring the liquid to a boil and cook over high heat until reduced and slightly syrupy.

Pour the sauce and figs over the chicken and serve hot.

OUT OF THE POT *Chicken Pan Bagnat (Niçoise Chicken Sandwich)*

Usually this salad-in-a-sandwich from Nice is made with canned tuna, but it is especially tasty with slow-cooked chicken. *Pan bagnat* means bathed bread, which is what you do with the anchovy dressing. Then the sandwich is pressed so that all the flavors can meld and get even better. You can make it in the morning and eat it when you get home from work. With some hard-cooked eggs and a good potato salad, it's my favorite picnic lunch to take to the beach.

SERVES 6

DRESSING
¾ cup olive oil
¼ cup fresh lemon juice
1 garlic clove, minced
1 tablespoon anchovy paste
½ teaspoon herbes de Provence
Salt and freshly ground pepper

2 loaves French or Italian bread
Herbed Roast Chicken with Garlic and Shallots (page 47)
Salt and freshly ground pepper
1 large tomato, thinly sliced
1 small red onion, thinly sliced

MAKE THE DRESSING: In a covered jar, combine the oil, lemon juice, garlic, anchovy paste, and herbs. Season with salt and pepper to taste. Shake well.

Cut the bread in half lengthwise. Scoop out some of the soft crumb from the inside of the bread. Drizzle half of the dressing over the inside of the bread.

Discard the chicken skin and bones and cut the meat into slices. Sprinkle the chicken with salt and pepper to taste. Arrange the chicken slices over the bottom half of the bread. Drizzle some of the remaining dressing over the chicken. Layer the tomato and onion slices on top. Drizzle with the remaining dressing and place the top on each loaf.

Wrap the loaves in aluminum foil. Place a cutting board or baking sheet on top and weight the sandwiches with heavy cans. Refrigerate for at least 2 hours or overnight.

About an hour before serving, remove the loaves from the refrigerator and bring to room temperature. Just before serving, cut each loaf into thirds.

Silky Chicken Liver Mousse

The gentle, moist heat of the slow cooker is perfect for cooking this chicken liver mousse. I adapted the recipe from one in *Made in Marseille,* by Daniel Young. Daniel uses evaporated milk instead of cream, which is perfect for the slow cooker since it does not curdle. Serve the mousse either unmolded or straight from the cooking vessel with an onion jam, as Daniel suggests, or with crackers or toasted French bread and cornichons for a great party appetizer.

SERVES 6

    Unsalted butter
2 **tablespoons olive oil**
8 **ounces chicken livers, tough sinews and fat trimmed**
¼ **cup chopped shallots**
1 **garlic clove, chopped**
2 **teaspoons chopped fresh thyme**
1 **12-ounce can evaporated whole milk**
4 **large egg yolks, beaten**
1 **teaspoon salt**
    Freshly ground pepper
    Fresh herb sprigs for garnish

Butter a 4-cup loaf pan or heatproof bowl or crock that will fit in the insert of a large slow cooker. Place a rack in the insert (to improvise one, see page 9).

In a medium skillet, heat the oil over medium-high heat. Add the chicken livers, shallots, garlic, and thyme. Cook until the livers are browned, about 3 minutes. Turn the livers over and cook for 1 to 2 minutes more, or until they are just slightly pink in the center.

Scrape the contents of the skillet into a food processor or blender. Add the evaporated milk, egg yolks, salt, and pepper to taste. Blend until very smooth. Strain the mixture into a bowl, pressing down on the solids.

Scrape the liver mixture into the prepared pan. Place the pan on the rack in the slow cooker. Carefully pour hot water around the pan to a depth of 1 inch.

Cover and cook on high for 2 hours, or until a knife inserted in the center comes out clean.

Remove the pan from the slow cooker. Let cool for 15 minutes on a wire rack. To unmold, run a knife around the inside of the pan and invert the mousse onto a serving plate. Cover and refrigerate until chilled. Serve garnished with fresh herbs.

Provençal Spinach Meatballs

Ground turkey and spinach meatballs take on a Provençal accent when flavored with orange zest and herbs and simmered in tomato sauce. Serve with noodles or rice for a satisfying dinner, or spoon onto toasted brioche rolls lined with arugula and top with some grated Gruyère for lunch.

SERVES 10

- 1 28-ounce can tomato puree
- ½ cup water
- 1 large shallot, thinly sliced
- 1 2-inch strip orange zest
- 1 teaspoon piment d'Espelette (see page 18) or paprika

  Salt and freshly ground pepper
- 1 10-ounce package frozen chopped spinach, thawed, or cooked and cooled fresh spinach
- 3 large eggs
- 1 garlic clove, minced
- 2½ pounds ground turkey
- ½ cup plain dry bread crumbs
- ½ teaspoon herbes de Provence
- ¼ cup all-purpose flour

Stir together the tomato puree, water, shallot, orange zest, and piment d'Espelette. Season with salt and pepper to taste. Pour half of the sauce into a large slow cooker.

Place the spinach in a towel and squeeze out as much of the liquid as possible.

Beat the eggs in a large bowl. Add the garlic, 1½ teaspoons salt, and pepper to taste. Add the spinach, turkey, bread crumbs, and herbs. Mix well and shape the mixture into 2-inch balls. Roll the meatballs lightly in the flour. Place the meatballs in the sauce. It's okay if you need to make a second layer. Pour the remaining sauce over the meatballs. Cover and cook on low for 4 to 6 hours, or until the meatballs are cooked through.

Stir well and serve hot.

Dijon-Style Cornish Hens with Mustard Sauce

The city of Dijon, in the Burgundy region of France, has been a center of mustard manufacturing since the thirteenth century. In this recipe, two kinds of mustard—smooth and coarse—give a tangy flavor boost to Cornish hens.

SERVES 2 TO 4

- 1 celery rib, chopped
- 1 large carrot, peeled and chopped
- 1 large red onion, sliced
- 2 Cornish game hens
  Salt and freshly ground pepper
- 2 garlic cloves
- ½ cup dry white wine
- 2 tablespoons Dijon mustard
- 2 tablespoons whole-grain mustard
- 2 tablespoons chopped fresh flat-leaf parsley
- 1 tablespoon unsalted butter

Scatter the vegetables in a large slow cooker. Sprinkle the hens inside and out with salt and pepper to taste. Tuck a garlic clove inside the cavity of each one. Place the hens in the slow cooker. Pour the wine around the hens. Cover and cook for 6 to 8 hours, or until the hens are tender and cooked through.

Remove the hens to a serving platter. Cover and keep warm.

Strain the cooking liquid into a medium saucepan. Bring the liquid to a boil and cook it over medium-high heat until slightly reduced. Turn the heat down slightly and whisk in the mustard.

Stir in the parsley and butter. Taste for seasoning. Pour the sauce over the hens and serve.

Duxelles–Stuffed Turkey Breast

Finely chopped mushrooms sautéed in butter are called *duxelles* in French. They are delicious as a topping for toasted bread or a filling for tartlets. Here the savory mixture is spread on boneless turkey breast, which is then rolled and tied like a roast.

When serving, spoon some of the turkey juices in the pot over the meat. If you prefer a thicker sauce, simmer the juices in a saucepan, stir in a tablespoon of cornstarch blended with 2 tablespoons cold cream or milk, and cook, stirring, until slightly thickened.

SERVES 6

DUXELLES

2 tablespoons unsalted butter

1 medium shallot, finely chopped

8 ounces white button mushrooms, finely chopped

Salt and freshly ground pepper

½ boneless turkey breast (about 2½ pounds)

Salt and freshly ground pepper

2 ounces sliced prosciutto or ham

3 medium carrots, peeled and thickly sliced

2 medium shallots or 1 large onion, thickly sliced

¼ cup chicken broth

MAKE THE DUXELLES: In a medium skillet, melt the butter over medium-high heat. Add the shallot and cook for 2 minutes, or until tender. Add the mushrooms and salt and pepper to taste. Cook, stirring often, until the liquid evaporates and the mushrooms are golden. Scrape the mixture into a bowl and let cool.

With a small, sharp knife, remove the skin from the turkey breast in one piece and set it aside. Starting at one long side, cut the breast almost in half lengthwise, stopping just short of the other side. Open the breast like a book. Flatten the meat with a mallet to an even thickness.

Sprinkle the turkey with salt and pepper to taste. Lay the prosciutto over the turkey. Spread the duxelles over the prosciutto. Roll up the turkey and tie the roll at 2-inch intervals with kitchen twine. Sprinkle with salt and pepper to taste. Spread the turkey skin over the rolled-up meat.

Scatter the carrots and shallots in a large slow cooker. Pour in the broth. Place the turkey roll on top. Cover and cook on high for 2 to 3 hours, or until an instant-read thermometer inserted into the center of the meat reads 165°F. Let cool slightly.

Slice the turkey and serve it with the braising liquid (see headnote) and vegetables.

Duck Confit

Confit is the French term for preserved spiced meats, usually duck, goose, or pork, slow cooked in fat until melt-in-your-mouth tender. Instead of extracting flavor the way water or broth would, the fat seals it in and protects the meat from drying out at the same time. A slow cooker makes perfect confit, since the temperature is controlled and the fat never overheats.

Stored in the refrigerator, confit keeps for weeks, so it is worth making a big batch. It is indispensable for adding authentic flavor to bean dishes like Cassoulet (page 110) or the cabbage and bean soup known as Garbure (page 39). You can also brown confit in a skillet and serve with a crisp green salad.

Duck or goose fat is typically used in confit. The most economical way to acquire the duck fat is by skimming off the fat from a roasting duck and saving it in the refrigerator or freezer until you have enough. You can also buy rendered duck fat at many butcher shops, in cans at gourmet shops, or online (see page 16). Or you can substitute chicken or goose fat or lard.

Duck fat makes the best sautéed potatoes you will ever eat.

SERVES 6

- 3 tablespoons kosher salt
- 2 large shallots, sliced
- 2 bay leaves
- 2 fresh thyme sprigs
- 2 teaspoons juniper berries (see page 17)
- 1 teaspoon whole peppercorns
- 6 skin-on whole duck legs (with thighs)
- 8 cups duck fat (see headnote)

In a large bowl, combine the salt, shallots, bay leaves, thyme, juniper berries, and peppercorns. Place the duck legs in the bowl and rub them all over with the salt mixture. Cover and refrigerate for 12 to 24 hours.

Place the duck fat in a large slow cooker. Cover and turn the heat to high.

When the fat is melted, rinse the duck legs and pat dry. Carefully place the legs in the melted fat. Turn the heat to low. Cover and cook for about 5 hours, or until the duck is very tender and the meat is coming away from the bones.

The duck can be eaten immediately or stored in the refrigerator.

TO STORE THE CONFIT: Turn off the heat and let the duck cool in the fat for 30 minutes. Have ready one or more clean containers. Transfer the duck to the containers. Strain the fat over the duck, using only the clear fat. (The cooking juices can be strained and added to soups, bean dishes, or stews.) Make sure that the duck is completely submerged in the fat. Cover and refrigerate for up to 1 month.

If you use only a portion of the confit at one time, keep the remaining pieces well covered with fat to preserve them. If you run out of duck fat, you can substitute a tasteless vegetable oil such as canola.

OUT OF THE POT *Crispy Duck Confit*

One summer my husband and I rented a vacation house in the Dordogne region, in southwest France. Confit duck was on the menu at every restaurant, either shredded into rillettes (see page 104 for a pork version) or cut up and tossed into a salad, a bean dish, or soup. Nothing beats duck leg confit crisped in a skillet and served with potatoes fried in duck fat and a green salad with vinaigrette.

SERVES 4

4 legs Duck Confit (page 72)

Preheat the oven to 400°F. Remove the duck legs from the fat and scrape off the excess fat. Heat a large ovenproof skillet over medium-high heat and add the legs, skin side down. Cook for 5 minutes, or until the skin is crisp and browned. Turn the legs and spoon off any excess fat in the pan. Transfer the pan to the oven and cook until the meat is heated through, about 5 minutes.

Serve hot.

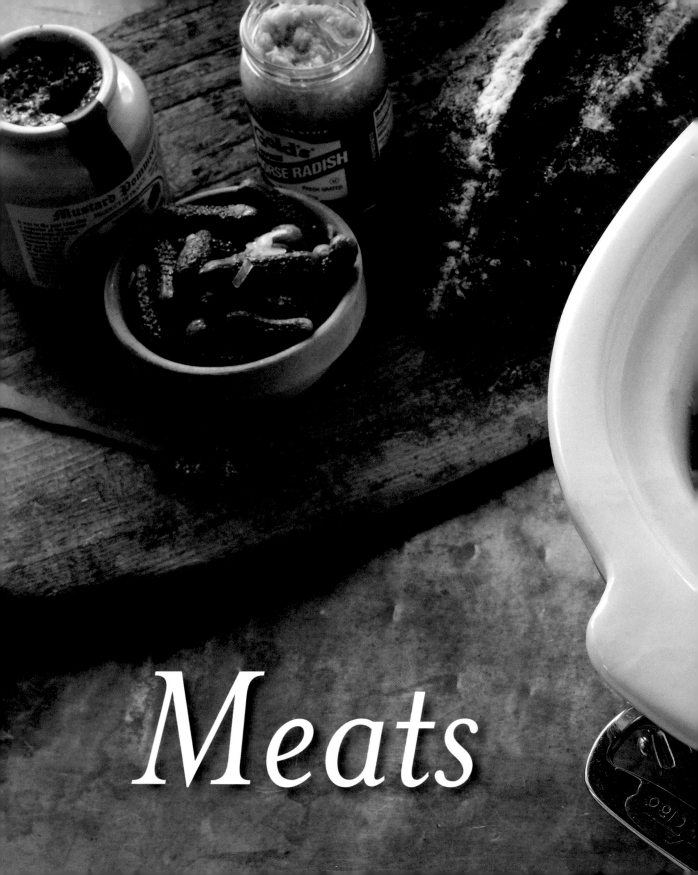

Meats

Meats

Red Wine–Braised Pot Roast 79

Bargemen's Beef Stew 81

Spiced Beef Brisket with Carrots and Turnips 82

Provençal Beef Stew with Black Olives..84

Beef Stew with Mushrooms, Rosemary, and Tomatoes.......................86

Short Ribs with Red Wine and Prunes 88

Short Ribs with Dark Beer and Shallots 90

Roussillon Meatballs 91

Meatballs Bayonnaise with Spicy Tomato and Pepper Sauce 92

Veal Blanquette (White Veal Stew) 94

Veal Shanks with Onion Sauce..96

Veal Marengo 97

Navarin Printanier (Lamb Stew with Spring Vegetables) 98

Lamb with Artichokes and Olives 100

Lamb Shanks with Lentils and Mustard 101

Lamb You Can Eat with a Spoon 102

Spicy Curried Pork 103

Rillettes (Spiced Potted Pork) 104

Country Pâté 107

Pork with Mushrooms and Cream 109

Cassoulet (Pork, Lamb, and Beans) 110

Normandy Pork with Apples 113

Choucroute Garni (Sausages with Sauerkraut) 114

Pork Ribs Hunter's Style 116

Red Wine–Braised Pot Roast

Simple and comforting, this French-style pot roast is a recipe I make all the time. Whether it's a meal for company or an everyday family dinner, it never fails to please. Dress it up with a buttery puree of potatoes and celeriac, or serve it simply with baked potatoes or buttered noodles.

SERVES 8

- 4 pounds boneless beef chuck, rump, or bottom round
  Salt and freshly ground pepper
- 2 tablespoons olive oil
- 3 large carrots, peeled and chopped
- 2 medium onions, chopped
- 2 celery ribs, chopped
- 2 garlic cloves, chopped
- 2 fresh thyme sprigs
- 1 bay leaf
  Pinch of ground cloves
- 2 cups dry red wine
- 2 cups Classic French Beef Broth (page 41) or store-bought beef broth
- 2 tablespoons cornstarch, blended with ¼ cup cool water

Pat the meat dry with paper towels. Sprinkle it with salt and pepper to taste. In a large skillet, heat the oil over medium-high heat. Add the beef and cook until nicely browned on all sides, about 15 minutes.

Scatter the carrots, onions, celery, garlic, herbs, and cloves in a large slow cooker. Place the beef on top. Pour the wine into the skillet and cook, scraping the bottom of the pan, until the wine comes to a simmer. Cook for 1 minute. Pour the wine over the beef. Add the broth to the slow cooker and season with salt and pepper to taste. Cover and cook on low for 8 to 10 hours, or until the beef is tender when pierced with a fork.

Remove the beef to a platter and cover to keep warm. Skim off the fat from the pan juices. To thicken the sauce, strain the cooking liquid into a saucepan and discard the solids. Bring the liquid to a simmer. Add the cornstarch mixture and cook, stirring, until smooth and slightly thickened, about 2 minutes. Taste for seasoning.

Slice the beef, spoon on the sauce, and serve.

Bargemen's Beef Stew

Traditionally, the men who operated shipping barges along the Rhône River would put on this stew to cook slowly while they went about their work. There is no liquid added, so the meat and onions cook in their own juices. When done, the beef is so tender that it practically melts. Stirring in a lively blend of anchovies, garlic, parsley, mustard, and vinegar just before serving gives the stew a zesty flavor. (The anchovies disappear into the sauce, leaving a mysterious tang.)

If you are making this stew ahead of time and reheating it, add the anchovy sauce at the last minute to retain its bright flavor.

SERVES 8

> Olive oil
>
> 4 pounds boneless beef chuck, well trimmed and cut into 1-inch cubes
>
> 3 tablespoons all-purpose flour
>
> Salt and freshly ground pepper
>
> 3 large onions, thinly sliced
>
> 6 anchovy fillets
>
> 6 garlic cloves, peeled
>
> ¼ cup chopped fresh flat-leaf parsley
>
> 2 tablespoons Dijon mustard
>
> 2 tablespoons red wine vinegar

Oil the insert of a large slow cooker. In a large bowl, toss the meat with the flour and salt and pepper to taste. Scatter half of the onions in the slow cooker. Add half of the meat. Add the remaining onions and top with the remaining meat. Cover and cook on low for 8 to 10 hours, or until the meat is very tender.

In a food processor or blender, chop the anchovies, garlic, and parsley very fine. Add the mustard and vinegar and pulse just until blended.

Skim the fat off the stew. Stir in the anchovy mixture. Taste for seasoning and serve.

Spiced Beef Brisket with Carrots and Turnips

Brisket, which comes from the breast area of the cow, is one of the toughest cuts of beef you can buy. But the good news is that it is ideal for the slow cooker, where it turns tender and remains moist.

Dark beer, brown sugar, mustard, and vinegar form a rich, tangy sauce for simmering the meat and vegetables. I like to serve the brisket with buttered wide noodles sprinkled with fresh parsley. If you have any leftovers, slice the meat thin and layer it on the bottom half of buttered French bread. Now dip the top in some of the tangy sauce for the best French dip sandwich you've ever had. Is a French dip sandwich really French? I've never seen anything like it in France. But that's okay—it's delicious, and that's reason enough to make this recipe.

SERVES 8

- 2 large onions, quartered
- 3 large carrots, peeled and each cut into 3 pieces
- 3 medium turnips, peeled and quartered
- 1 3½- to 4-pound beef brisket, trimmed
  Salt and freshly ground pepper
- 2 tablespoons olive oil
- 1 12-ounce bottle dark beer
- 2 tablespoons dark brown sugar
- 2 tablespoons red wine vinegar
- 2 tablespoons Dijon mustard
- ¼ teaspoon ground cinnamon

Place the onions, carrots, and turnips in a large slow cooker.

Pat the meat dry with paper towels. Sprinkle it with salt and pepper to taste. Heat the oil in a large skillet. Add the beef and brown it well on both sides, about 15 minutes. Place the beef on top of the vegetables in the slow cooker.

Add the beer, sugar, vinegar, mustard, and cinnamon to the skillet and cook, scraping the bottom of the pan, until the liquid comes to a simmer. Add salt and pepper to taste. Pour the liquid over the brisket.

Cover and cook on low for 8 hours, or until the meat is very tender when pierced with a fork.

Slice the beef, spoon the sauce over the meat and vegetables, and serve.

Provençal Beef Stew with Black Olives

Even if I didn't know where this stew originated, the sunny flavors of the tomatoes, orange zest, and black olives—signature ingredients of Provence—would give it away.

SERVES 8

- 4 pounds boneless beef chuck, well trimmed and cut into 2-inch pieces
- ¼ cup all-purpose flour
- Salt and freshly ground pepper
- 2 ounces salt pork or bacon, cut into small dice
- 1 tablespoon olive oil
- ½ cup dry white wine
- 5 garlic cloves, peeled
- 2 medium onions, chopped
- 1 cup chopped canned tomatoes
- 2 fresh thyme sprigs or ½ teaspoon dried thyme
- 2 2-inch strips orange zest
- 1 bay leaf
- ½ cup beef broth
- 1 cup imported black olives, pitted
- ¼ cup chopped fresh flat-leaf parsley

Pat the beef dry with paper towels. In a bowl, combine the flour with salt and pepper to taste. Add the beef, a few pieces at a time, and toss until lightly coated.

Put the salt pork and olive oil in a large skillet and cook over medium heat, stirring often, until the pork is golden brown on all sides, about 7 minutes. With a slotted spoon, transfer the pork to a large slow cooker.

Add the meat to the skillet in batches, without crowding the pan. Brown the beef well on all sides, about 20 minutes total. Transfer the beef to the slow cooker.

Add the wine to the skillet and cook, scraping the bottom of the pan to release the browned bits. Bring the liquid to a boil and cook for 1 minute. Pour the liquid into the slow cooker.

Add the remaining ingredients except the olives and parsley. Cover and cook on low for 8 to 10 hours, or until the beef is tender when pierced with a fork. Add the olives and cover and cook for 15 minutes more.

Skim off the fat and discard the bay leaf. Serve hot, sprinkled with the parsley.

Beef Stew with Mushrooms, Rosemary, and Tomatoes

In France, this stew is known as *boeuf en daube* because it is cooked in a stew pot known as a *daubière.* The slow cooker is my new equivalent. Using a variety of mushrooms makes the stew even more enticing.

SERVES 8

4 pounds boneless beef chuck, well trimmed and cut into 2-inch pieces
½ cup all-purpose flour
   Salt and freshly ground pepper
¼ cup olive oil
2 medium onions, chopped
4 garlic cloves, chopped
1 tablespoon tomato paste
1 cup dry red wine
2 cups Classic French Beef Broth (page 41) or store-bought beef broth
4 medium carrots, peeled and sliced ¼ inch thick
1 cup chopped canned tomatoes
1 fresh rosemary sprig
1 bay leaf
2 tablespoons unsalted butter
1 pound white button mushrooms, quartered
2 tablespoons chopped fresh flat-leaf parsley

Pat the beef dry with paper towels. In a bowl, combine the flour with salt and pepper to taste. Add the beef, a few pieces at a time, and toss until lightly coated.

    Heat the oil in a large skillet. Add the beef in batches and cook until browned on all sides, about 20 minutes total. Place the meat in a large slow cooker.

    Add the onions to the skillet and cook until softened, about 5 minutes. Stir in the garlic and tomato paste. Add the wine and cook, scraping the pan, until the liquid comes to a simmer. Pour the contents of the skillet over the meat. Add the broth, carrots, tomatoes, and herbs to the slow cooker. Cover and cook on low for 8 hours, or until the beef is tender when pierced with a fork.

When the beef is almost ready, melt the butter in a medium skillet over medium-high heat. Add the mushrooms and salt and pepper to taste. Cook, stirring often, until the mushrooms are golden, about 10 minutes.

Stir the mushrooms into the stew and discard the bay leaf. Serve hot, sprinkled with the parsley.

Short Ribs with Red Wine and Prunes

No one will ever guess that the sauce in this recipe owes its sweet, rich flavor to the prunes. Serve the ribs and sauce with egg noodles.

SERVES 8

- 4 pounds bone-in beef short ribs, well trimmed
- Salt and freshly ground pepper
- ⅓ cup all-purpose flour
- ¼ cup olive oil
- 2 medium onions, chopped
- 2 medium carrots, peeled and chopped
- 2 celery ribs, chopped
- 6 large garlic cloves, chopped
- 1 teaspoon herbes de Provence
- 2 bay leaves
- 1 cup dry red wine
- 3 tablespoons tomato paste
- ½ cup chopped pitted prunes
- 4 cups Classic French Beef Broth (page 41) or store-bought beef broth
- 2 tablespoons Dijon mustard
- 2 tablespoons chopped fresh flat-leaf parsley

Sprinkle the ribs with salt and pepper to taste. Roll the ribs in the flour and tap off the excess.

In a large heavy skillet, heat the oil over medium heat. Cook the ribs in batches, turning them occasionally, until browned on all sides, about 20 minutes total. Transfer the browned ribs to a large slow cooker.

Add the onions, carrots, and celery to the skillet and cook, stirring often, until golden, about 15 minutes. Stir in the garlic and herbs and cook for 1 minute more. Add the wine and cook, scraping the bottom of the pan, until the wine comes to a boil. Cook for 1 minute. Stir in the tomato paste, prunes, and broth. Pour the contents of the skillet over the ribs.

Cover and cook on low for 8 to 10 hours, or until the ribs are tender and the meat is coming away from the bones. Skim off the fat from the surface of the liquid. Stir in the mustard and discard the bay leaves. Taste for seasoning. Sprinkle with the chopped parsley and serve.

Short Ribs with Dark Beer and Shallots

The sweetness of the shallots and the tartness of the vinegar balance the flavors of the beer and beef in this simple recipe. Serve it with mashed potatoes and broccoli.

SERVES 6 TO 8

5	pounds bone-in beef short ribs, well trimmed
	Salt and freshly ground pepper
1	tablespoon bacon fat or vegetable oil
3–4	large shallots, cut into ¼-inch slices (about 1 cup)
1	16-ounce bottle dark beer
¼	cup red wine vinegar or sherry vinegar
2	tablespoons tomato paste

Pat the ribs dry with paper towels. Sprinkle them with salt and pepper to taste.

In a large skillet, melt the bacon fat or heat the oil over medium-high heat. Brown the ribs in batches, turning them occasionally, about 20 minutes total. Transfer them to a large slow cooker.

Pour off most of the fat in the skillet. Stir in the shallots and cook until lightly golden. Add the beer, vinegar, and tomato paste. Bring the liquid to a simmer, scraping the bottom of the pan. Pour the liquid over the ribs in the slow cooker. Cover and cook on low for 8 hours, or until the ribs are very tender.

Remove the ribs from the slow cooker and cover to keep warm. Skim the fat from the cooking liquid. Pour the liquid into a saucepan and cook over medium-high heat until it is slightly reduced. Spoon the sauce over the ribs and serve hot.

Roussillon Meatballs

A town in southern France near the Spanish border, Roussillon is famous for delicious meatballs made with beef, pork, and olives. A tiny bit of cinnamon gives this dish a special flavor and aroma. I like to serve the meatballs and sauce over egg noodles, accompanied by buttered peas.

SERVES 6 TO 8

- 1 28-ounce can tomato puree
- ½ cup water
- 2 scallions, minced
- 2 teaspoons salt
- 2 pinches of ground cinnamon
- ½ cup all-purpose flour
- 1 pound ground beef chuck
- 1 pound ground pork
- ¾ cup crumbled French or Italian bread, soaked in water and lightly squeezed
- 2 garlic cloves, finely chopped
- 2 tablespoons chopped fresh flat-leaf parsley, plus more for garnish
- 2 large eggs
- Freshly ground pepper
- 1 cup chopped pitted green olives

Stir together the tomato puree, water, scallions, ½ teaspoon of the salt, and the cinnamon. Pour half the sauce into a large slow cooker.

Spread the flour on a piece of wax paper.

In a large bowl, mix the meats, bread, garlic, parsley, eggs, the remaining 1½ teaspoons salt, and pepper to taste. Moisten your hands and roll the meat mixture into 2-inch balls. Lightly roll the meatballs in the flour.

Add the meatballs to the slow cooker. Pour on the remaining sauce. Cover and cook on low for 4 to 5 hours, until the meatballs are cooked through. Just before serving, stir the meatballs in the sauce and add the olives. Serve hot, garnished with parsley.

Meatballs Bayonnaise with Spicy Tomato and Pepper Sauce

The city of Bayonne, in the Basque region of France, is known for its tradition of chocolate-making, but when I think of Bayonne, I remember these wonderful meatballs. Two herbs, cumin and marjoram, give them a unique flavor, and the slightly spicy pepper and tomato sauce is the perfect accompaniment. Serve the meatballs and sauce with white rice and some kale sautéed with olive oil and garlic, or enjoy them in a sandwich.

SERVES 6

- 1 28-ounce can tomato puree
- 2 red bell peppers, seeded and chopped
- 1 medium onion, finely chopped
-    Salt
-    Pinch of crushed red pepper
- 1 bay leaf
- ¾ cup crumbled French or Italian bread
- ¼ cup milk
- ⅓ cup all-purpose flour
- 2 pounds ground beef chuck
- 2 tablespoons chopped fresh flat-leaf parsley
- 2 garlic cloves, minced
- 1 large egg
- 1 teaspoon ground cumin
- ½ teaspoon dried marjoram
-    Freshly ground pepper

Stir together the tomato puree, peppers, onion, 1 teaspoon salt, crushed pepper, and bay leaf. Pour half of the sauce into a large slow cooker.

In a small bowl, soak the bread in the milk for a few minutes. Lightly squeeze the bread and discard the milk. Spread the flour on a piece of wax paper.

In a large bowl, mix together the soaked bread, ground beef, parsley, garlic, egg, cumin, marjoram, 1½ teaspoons salt, and pepper to taste. Moisten your hands and shape the mixture into 2-inch balls. Lightly roll the meatballs in the flour.

Transfer the meatballs to the slow cooker and top with the remaining sauce. Cover and cook on low for 4 to 5 hours, or until the meatballs are cooked through. Discard the bay leaf and serve hot.

Veal Blanquette (White Veal Stew)

For this refined stew, the meat, instead of being browned, is blanched—dropped briefly into boiling water to give it a pale color and delicate texture. This step might seem like extra work, but the end result is well worth the time. You can even start the stew a day ahead and finish it up just before serving.

The flavors of the meat, mushrooms, and pearl onions are subtle and sophisticated. Serve the stew with boiled potatoes or wide noodles.

SERVES 8

Salt

3 pounds boneless veal chuck or shoulder, trimmed and cut into 2-inch chunks

1 medium carrot, peeled and left whole

1 medium onion, peeled and left whole

1 celery rib, left whole

1 garlic clove, chopped

2 fresh thyme sprigs

4 cups Chicken Broth (page 40) or store-bought chicken broth

24 frozen pearl onions, partially thawed

8 ounces white button mushrooms, quartered

2 tablespoons cornstarch

½ cup heavy cream

1 tablespoon fresh lemon juice

Chopped fresh flat-leaf parsley

Bring a large pot of water to a boil. Add 1 teaspoon salt. Add half of the veal pieces. Cover the pot and bring the water back to a boil. Cook for 2 minutes. With a slotted spoon, transfer the veal to a bowl. Blanch the remaining meat in the same way. Rinse the meat under cool water and drain well.

Place the veal, carrot, onion, celery, garlic, and thyme in a large slow cooker. Add the broth, cover, and cook on low for 4 hours.

Stir in the pearl onions and mushrooms and cover and cook for 1 hour more, or until the veal is very tender.

Remove the veal, vegetables, and mushrooms from the slow cooker with a slotted spoon and place them in a large bowl. Discard the carrot, whole onion, and celery rib. Pour the liquid into a large Dutch oven set over high heat and boil until the liquid is reduced to about 3 cups.

In a small bowl, blend together the cornstarch and cream. Stir the mixture into the Dutch oven and simmer until the sauce is slightly thickened. Add the lemon juice. Stir in the veal, mushrooms, and pearl onions. Reheat gently and taste for seasoning.

Serve hot, sprinkled with the parsley.

Veal Shanks with Onion Sauce

Italian cooks aren't the only ones who make *osso buco*. Here is a French version with a rich onion and garlic sauce. The garlic cloves are left whole in their skins so that you can squeeze them out and mash them into the sauce to eat with the meat. This is great with a rice pilaf and a bottle of Beaujolais.

SERVES 6

⅓ cup all-purpose flour

Salt and freshly ground pepper

6 1½-inch-thick slices veal shank

¼ cup olive oil

3 large onions, halved and thinly sliced

3 medium carrots, peeled and thickly sliced

½ cup dry white wine

12 garlic cloves, unpeeled

2 tablespoons tomato paste

1 cup Classic French Beef Broth (page 41) or store-bought beef broth

1 bay leaf

½ teaspoon chopped fresh thyme

2 tablespoons chopped fresh flat-leaf parsley

Toss together the flour and salt and pepper to taste. Roll the veal slices in the flour, tapping off the excess. In a large skillet, heat the oil over medium heat. Add the veal in batches and brown well on both sides, about 20 minutes total. Transfer the browned meat to a large slow cooker.

Add the onions and carrots to the skillet and cook, stirring occasionally, until golden, about 10 minutes. Add the wine to the skillet and cook, scraping the bottom of the pan, until the liquid comes to a boil. Remove any loose skin from the garlic, but do not peel. Add the garlic, tomato paste, broth, bay leaf, and thyme to the skillet and stir to combine. Pour the contents of the skillet over the meat.

Cover and cook on low for 5 to 6 hours, or until the meat is very tender. Discard the bay leaf, sprinkle with the parsley, and serve.

Veal Marengo

The Battle of Marengo in 1800 was a decisive victory for Napoleon over the invading Austrians. When the fighting ended, the cooks for the French forces scrambled to make a meal out of whatever ingredients were available in the region. The result was a big hit, and nowadays Marengo-style dishes continue to be popular in bistros all over France. This simplified slow cooker version is made with veal, tomatoes, olives, wine, and some orange zest for a sunny flavor. Serve with slices of toasted French bread to soak up the tasty sauce.

SERVES 8

⅓ cup all-purpose flour

Salt and freshly ground pepper

3 pounds boneless veal shoulder, trimmed and cut into 2-inch cubes

¼ cup olive oil

1 medium onion, finely chopped

2 garlic cloves, finely chopped

1 cup dry white wine

1 cup chopped canned tomatoes

2 tablespoons tomato paste

1 cup Classic French Beef Broth (page 41) or store-bought beef broth

1 2-inch strip orange zest

12 small imported black olives, pitted

2 tablespoons chopped fresh basil

Combine the flour and salt and pepper to taste on a piece of wax paper. Roll the veal pieces in the flour, tapping off the excess. Transfer the meat to a large slow cooker.

Heat the oil over medium heat in a large skillet and add the onion and garlic. Cook, stirring often, until tender, about 5 minutes. Add the wine and bring to a simmer. Stir in the tomatoes and tomato paste. Pour the wine mixture over the meat in the slow cooker. Add the broth.

Cover and cook on low for 5 to 6 hours, or until the veal is tender. Add the orange zest and olives and cover and cook for 30 minutes more. Stir in the basil and serve hot.

Navarin Printanier
(Lamb Stew with Spring Vegetables)

When winter turns to spring, I start to crave this stew made with tender lamb and a gardenful of vegetables. It is beautiful and delectable—just the thing to chase away the last blast of winter. Sometimes I add green beans or asparagus along with the peas and onions. It really doesn't need anything else, except some good bread to soak up the sauce.

SERVES 8

- 6 medium waxy potatoes, such as Yukon Gold, peeled and cut into 1-inch pieces
- 4 medium carrots, peeled and cut into 1-inch pieces
- 4 medium turnips, peeled and each cut into 8 wedges
- 4 pounds boneless lamb shoulder, trimmed and cut into 2-inch pieces
- ¼ cup all-purpose flour
- Salt and freshly ground pepper
- 2 tablespoons olive oil
- 2 cups Chicken Broth (page 40) or store-bought chicken broth
- ⅓ cup tomato paste
- 3 garlic cloves, minced
- ½ teaspoon chopped fresh thyme
- 1 bay leaf
- 16 frozen pearl onions, partially thawed
- 1 cup frozen peas, partially thawed

Scatter the potatoes, carrots, and turnips in a large slow cooker.

On a piece of wax paper, toss the lamb with the flour and salt and pepper to taste. In a large skillet, heat the oil over medium heat. Add to the pan only as many pieces of the lamb as will fit comfortably without crowding. Cook until nicely browned on all sides, about 20 minutes total. Transfer the meat to the slow cooker and brown the remaining lamb.

Pour any fat out of the pan. Add the broth and bring to a simmer, scraping the bottom of the pan. Stir in the tomato paste, garlic, and thyme. Bring the liquid to a simmer and pour it over the lamb. Add the bay leaf.

Cover and cook on low for 6 hours, or until the lamb is tender. Add the onions and peas and cover and cook for 30 minutes more. Discard the bay leaf and serve hot.

Lamb with Artichokes and Olives

In the springtime, cooks in most European countries prepare lamb with artichokes, and French cooks are no exception. The sweet flavor of the artichokes complements the succulent meat, and the olives add a salty flavor. Serve this simple stew with Polenta with Sheep's-Milk Cheese and Crème Fraîche (page 184).

SERVES 6

- 3 pounds boneless lamb shoulder, trimmed and cut into 2-inch pieces
- Salt and freshly ground pepper
- 2 garlic cloves, finely chopped
- ½ cup dry white wine or chicken broth
- 2 tablespoons fresh lemon juice
- 1 10-ounce package frozen artichoke hearts, thawed
- 1 cup imported black olives, pitted
- 2 tablespoons chopped fresh flat-leaf parsley

Sprinkle the lamb with salt and pepper to taste. Place the lamb in a large slow cooker. Scatter the garlic over the meat. Add the wine and lemon juice.

Cover and cook on low for 5 to 6 hours, or until the lamb is tender when pierced with a fork. Add the artichoke hearts and olives and baste them with the hot juices. Turn the heat to high and cover and cook for 30 minutes more, or until the artichokes are tender.

Sprinkle with the parsley and serve hot.

Lamb Shanks with Lentils and Mustard

The lentils in this recipe melt into a thick puree during the long, slow cooking, making a perfect base for the tender lamb shanks.

SERVES 6

- 6 small lamb shanks (about 5 pounds), trimmed
  Salt and freshly ground pepper
- 1 pound brown lentils, rinsed and picked over
- 3 medium carrots, peeled and thickly sliced
- 1 celery rib, chopped
- 1 large onion, chopped
- 2 large garlic cloves, chopped
- 1 cup chopped fresh or canned tomatoes
- 1 bay leaf
- 3 cups Classic French Beef Broth (page 41) or store-bought beef broth
- ½ cup dry red wine
- 3 tablespoons Dijon mustard
- 2 tablespoons chopped fresh rosemary
  Chopped fresh flat-leaf parsley

Sprinkle the lamb shanks with salt and pepper to taste.

In a large slow cooker, combine the lentils, carrots, celery, onion, garlic, tomatoes, and bay leaf. Place the shanks in the cooker, pressing them into the lentils and vegetables. Stir together the broth, wine, mustard, rosemary, and salt and pepper to taste and add this mixture to the cooker.

Cover and cook on low for 8 to 10 hours, or until the lentils are very tender and the meat is coming away from the bone. Remove the bay leaf. Sprinkle with parsley and serve hot.

Lamb You Can Eat with a Spoon

Sometimes called "seven-hour leg of lamb," which is about how long it takes to cook in a low oven, this traditional French dish has been around for a few hundred years. The meat practically melts into the flavorful cooking juices, and the aroma of the lamb, garlic, and flavorings is intoxicating. I love to serve this with flageolets or French-style white beans, which soak up the lamb cooking juices.

A word of advice: before buying the meat for this recipe, check the dimensions of your slow cooker to be sure it will fit.

SERVES 6 TO 8

- 6 large garlic cloves, chopped
- 4 medium onions, chopped
- 4 large carrots, peeled and chopped
- 1 cup chopped canned tomatoes
- 3 fresh thyme sprigs
- 2 bay leaves
- 1 4-pound boneless shank-end leg of lamb, rolled and tied
  Salt and freshly ground pepper
- 2 tablespoons olive oil
- 1 cup dry white wine
- 2 cups Classic French Beef Broth (page 41) or store-bought beef broth

Scatter the garlic, onions, carrots, tomatoes, and herbs in a large slow cooker.

Sprinkle the lamb with salt and pepper to taste. Heat the oil in a large skillet over medium heat. Add the lamb and brown it on all sides, about 15 minutes.

Place the lamb on top of the vegetables in the cooker. Add the wine to the skillet and stir, scraping up the browned bits from the bottom of the pan. Pour the wine and the broth over the lamb.

Cover and cook on low for 8 to 10 hours, or until the meat is very tender.

Transfer the lamb to a serving dish and cover to keep warm. Strain the juices from the slow cooker and discard the solids. Skim off the fat and adjust the seasonings. Break the meat into chunks. Spoon the cooking liquid over and serve hot.

Spicy Curried Pork

A friend told me about a great little bistro near the Sorbonne, in Paris. The place was packed with students and instructors tucking into all kinds of delicious-looking food. I ordered the day's special, a spicy curried pork stew, which was served with buttered rice. It was so good that I ate every bit of it. This is my version of that stew, made with chunks of pork shoulder. It's a perfect cut for stewing and braising because it has enough fat to prevent the meat from drying out.

SERVES 6

¼ cup olive oil

3½ pounds boneless pork shoulder, trimmed and cut into 1-inch pieces

1 medium onion, finely chopped

1 medium carrot, peeled and finely chopped

2 large garlic cloves, finely chopped

1 tablespoon curry powder

½ cup beef broth

1½ cups tomato puree (one 10.75-ounce can)

½ teaspoon piment d'Espelette (see page 18) or cayenne

Salt

In a large skillet, heat the oil over medium heat. Pat the pork dry with paper towels. Add the pork to the skillet in batches and cook until lightly browned, about 20 minutes total. Remove the pork to a large slow cooker.

Spoon off all but 2 tablespoons of the fat from the skillet. Add the onion and carrot to the skillet and cook until the onion is golden, about 10 minutes. Add the garlic and curry powder and cook for 2 minutes more, stirring often. Add the broth and stir well, scraping the bottom of the pan. Pour the mixture over the pork.

Stir in the tomato puree, piment d'Espelette, and salt to taste. Cover and cook on low for 5 to 6 hours, or until the pork is tender. Serve hot.

Rillettes (Spiced Potted Pork)

A meal in a French bistro frequently begins with a little pot of rillettes: spiced, slow-cooked pork shredded into a spreadable pâté that is served on slices of toasted baguette. The slow cooker maintains the even low temperature needed to cook the meat perfectly. After it cools, the meat is shredded or mashed until it is smooth, packed into crocks, and sealed with a layer of fat. It keeps in the refrigerator for 2 weeks (and in the freezer for 2 months). I like to make a batch of rillettes just before the holidays to have on hand for a party appetizer, meals, or just a snack.

MAKES 4 CUPS

- 3 pounds boneless pork shoulder or boneless butt, cut into 1-inch pieces
- 8 ounces pork fat back, cut into 1-inch chunks
- 6 garlic cloves, halved
- 2 fresh thyme sprigs
- 1 bay leaf
- 1 tablespoon coarse salt
- 1 teaspoon freshly ground pepper
- ¼ teaspoon ground allspice
- ¼ teaspoon ground cinnamon
- ½ cup dry white wine
- ½ cup water
- Cornichons or pickled vegetables and thin slices toasted French bread for serving

Place the pork and fat back in a large slow cooker and add the garlic, thyme, bay leaf, salt, pepper, spices, wine, and water. Stir to combine. Cover and cook on high for about 1 hour, until the fat is melted. Reduce the heat to low and cook for 8 hours, or until the meat is very tender and falling apart.

Let the meat cool slightly in the slow cooker. Discard the bay leaf and thyme. Remove the meat with a slotted spoon and place it in a large bowl. Strain the liquid, reserving it, and discard the solids. Skim off the fat and reserve it separately.

With an electric mixer, preferably a stand mixer with the flat beater attachment, mix the meat on low speed until it shreds. (You can also shred the meat with two forks or pound it in a mortar and pestle. Don't use a blender or food processor, though—you don't want the meat to turn into a puree.) Add some of the reserved cooking liquid to make a light, creamy paste. Taste for seasoning. Pack the mixture into small crocks or ramekins. Refrigerate until chilled, about 2 hours.

Reheat the fat until it becomes liquid. Pour a little over each of the crocks to seal. Cover the crocks with plastic wrap and refrigerate for up to 2 weeks or freeze for up to 2 months.

When ready to serve, remove the rillettes from the refrigerator or freezer and let come to room temperature. Serve with the cornichons or pickled vegetables and toasted French bread.

Country Pâté

A sumptuous blend of meats and seasonings, a country pâté is the ultimate picnic food and is great for a party appetizer or when served with a green salad and potato salad for a fabulous lunch. It is no more difficult to make than meat loaf. And, just like meat loaf, it makes a darn good sandwich too.

SERVES 12

- 2 tablespoons bacon fat or butter
- 1 cup finely chopped onion
- 8 ounces sliced bacon
- 1 pound ground pork
- 1 pound ground turkey
- 8 ounces chicken livers, tough sinews and fat trimmed, finely chopped
- ½ cup fresh bread crumbs
- 2 garlic cloves, minced
- 1 large egg
- 2 teaspoons salt
- ½ teaspoon dried thyme
- ¼ teaspoon freshly ground pepper
- ¼ teaspoon ground allspice
- 3 tablespoons brandy or cognac

  Grainy mustard, cornichons, and thin slices toasted French bread for serving

In a small skillet, melt the bacon fat over medium heat. Add the onion and cook, stirring often, until tender and golden, about 8 minutes. Let cool.

Line the sides and bottom of a 9-x-5-x-3-inch loaf pan by placing the slices of bacon crosswise and overlapping slightly. Reserve 3 slices for the top.

In a large bowl, combine the cooked onion with the remaining ingredients, except for the serving ingredients. Mix well. Spoon the mixture into the prepared pan, pressing it lightly. Smooth the surface and place the 3 reserved bacon slices lengthwise on top.

Place a small rack in the insert of a large slow cooker (to improvise one, see page 9). Place the pan on the rack. Cover and cook on high for 5 hours, or until the temperature on an instant-read thermometer reads 165°F.

Remove the pâté and let cool slightly. Cover and refrigerate for at least 8 hours before slicing. The pâté can be kept for up to 5 days in the refrigerator or frozen for up to 2 months.

Serve with grainy mustard, cornichons, and toasted French bread.

Pork with Mushrooms and Cream

Pork, shallots, mushrooms, and cream make this stew ideal for a special occasion. Serve it with buttered noodles and a green vegetable.

SERVES 6 TO 8

- 8 ounces white button mushrooms, thickly sliced
- 2 tablespoons unsalted butter
- 1 tablespoon vegetable oil
- 3½ pounds boneless pork shoulder, trimmed and cut into 2-inch chunks
- ½ cup chopped shallots
- 1 cup Chicken Broth (page 40) or store-bought chicken broth
- ½ teaspoon herbes de Provence
  Salt and freshly ground pepper
- ½ cup heavy cream or crème fraîche (see page 14)
- 2 tablespoons chopped fresh flat-leaf parsley

Scatter the mushrooms in a large slow cooker.

In a large skillet, melt the butter with the oil over medium-high heat. Pat the pork dry with paper towels and brown it in batches on all sides, about 20 minutes total. Transfer the pork to the slow cooker.

Add the shallots to the skillet and cook for 2 minutes, or until softened. Add the broth, herbes de Provence, and salt and pepper to taste. Bring the liquid to a simmer, scraping the bottom of the pan. Cook for 1 minute. Pour the liquid over the pork and mushrooms. Cover and cook on low for 6 hours, or until the pork is tender.

With a slotted spoon, remove the meat and mushrooms from the slow cooker to a large bowl and cover to keep warm. Pour the liquid into a saucepan and skim off the fat. Bring the liquid to a boil and add the cream. Cook until the sauce is slightly thickened, about 2 minutes. Taste for seasoning. Pour the sauce over the pork and mushrooms. Sprinkle with the parsley and serve hot.

Cassoulet (Pork, Lamb, and Beans)

Garlicky pork sausage, lamb, beans, and duck confit simmered together in an aromatic broth are the makings of the soul-warming stew known as cassoulet. A full-fledged cassoulet is magnificent, but the traditional version takes several days of cooking to complete.

Today I make it this easy way. If I don't have my own homemade duck confit, I use store-bought, which is readily available, or even fresh chicken thighs.

SERVES 8 TO 10

- 1 pound dried navy beans, pea beans, or other small white beans, rinsed and picked over
- 2 medium carrots, peeled and thickly sliced
- 6 garlic cloves, finely chopped
- 1 bay leaf
- 4 ounces bacon or pancetta, cut into ½-inch strips
- 1 large onion, finely chopped
- 2 tablespoons tomato paste
- 4 cups Classic French Beef Broth (page 41) or store-bought beef broth
- 2 pounds boneless lamb shoulder, trimmed and cut into 2-inch pieces
- 1 pound kielbasa or other garlic sausage, cut into serving pieces
- 2 legs Duck Confit (page 72) or 4 bone-in chicken thighs
- 1 teaspoon salt
  Freshly ground pepper
  About 1 cup panko (Japanese bread crumbs) or plain dry bread crumbs
- 3 cups Croutons (page 216)

Soak the beans in water to cover by several inches for 4 hours or overnight or quick-soak them (see page 16). Drain the beans and place them in a large slow cooker. Add the carrots, garlic, and bay leaf.

In a medium skillet over medium heat, cook the bacon until golden. Add the onion and cook, stirring often, until tender. Stir in the tomato paste and 1 cup of the broth. Bring the mixture to a simmer.

Arrange the lamb, kielbasa, and duck legs on top of the beans in the slow cooker. Add the contents of the skillet, the remaining 3 cups broth, the salt, and pepper to taste.

Cover and cook on low for 8 to 10 hours, or until the beans and meat are very tender.

Place the panko in a small skillet and toast over medium heat, stirring occasionally, until lightly browned.

With a spoon, skim off the fat from the cooking liquid. Remove the bay leaf. Stir in enough of the panko to thicken the cooking liquid. Scatter the croutons on top and serve hot.

Normandy Pork with Apples

In this Norman-style dish, pork is slow cooked with apples, apple cider, and apple cider vinegar and finished with a bit of cream. Hot buttered noodles are the perfect companion.

SERVES 8

- 4 large, firm cooking apples, such as Fuji or Golden Delicious
- 12 ounces shallots (about 6 large)
- 2 tablespoons unsalted butter
- 2 tablespoons vegetable oil
- 3 pounds boneless pork shoulder, trimmed and cut into 2-inch pieces
  Salt and freshly ground pepper
- 1 cup apple cider or apple juice
- ¼ cup apple cider vinegar
- ½ cup chicken broth
- ½ cup crème fraîche (see page 14) or sour cream

Cut the apples into quarters. Remove the cores and stems but leave the skin intact. Place the apples in a large slow cooker.

Trim off the ends of the shallots and peel off the skins. If the shallots have more than one section, separate them. Place the shallots in the slow cooker.

In a large skillet, melt the butter with the oil over medium heat. Pat the pork pieces dry with paper towels. Brown the pork in batches, about 20 minutes total. Add the pork to the slow cooker. Sprinkle with salt and pepper to taste.

Pour off the fat in the skillet. Add the apple cider and vinegar and cook, stirring, until the liquid comes to a simmer. Stir in the broth, scraping the bottom of the pan. Pour the liquid over the pork, shallots, and apples. Cover and cook on low for 8 hours, or until the pork is very tender.

Just before serving, remove the pork, apples, and shallots with a slotted spoon and place in a large bowl. Cover and keep warm.

Skim the fat from the juices in the slow cooker. Stir in the crème fraîche and taste for seasoning. Pour the sauce over all. Serve hot.

Choucroute Garni
(Sausages with Sauerkraut)

Sauerkraut simmered with potatoes and a variety of sausages is about as simple and delicious as a meal can be. You can vary the meats and sausages according to what is available. Knockwurst, weisswurst, and garlic sausage are good, or try smoked ham hocks or slab bacon.

In Alsace, *choucroute* is served with black bread, mustard, horseradish, and pickles, along with some Alsatian Riesling or Gewürztraminer. It's a great meal for a party.

SERVES 6 TO 8

- 2 pounds sauerkraut
- 6 medium waxy potatoes, such as Yukon Gold, peeled and quartered
- 1 large onion, sliced
- 1 large carrot, peeled and cut into ½-inch slices
- 6 garlic cloves, unpeeled
- 10 juniper berries (see page 17), lightly crushed
- 1 teaspoon caraway seeds
- 2 whole cloves
- 3 fresh thyme sprigs
- 2 bay leaves
- 6 cooked bratwursts
- 1 pound kielbasa, cut into 2-inch pieces
- 4 smoked pork chops or 2 smoked ham hocks
- 1 cup dry white wine
  Dijon mustard, cornichons, and prepared horseradish for serving

Rinse the sauerkraut well in a colander under cool running water. Squeeze the sauerkraut to remove the liquid.

Place half of the sauerkraut in a large slow cooker, separating the pieces with your fingers. Add the potatoes, onion, carrot, garlic, juniper berries, caraway seeds, cloves, thyme, and bay leaves. Arrange the remaining sauerkraut on top.

Push the sausages and pork chops down into the sauerkraut. Add the wine. Cover and cook on low for 8 hours, or until the potatoes are tender.

Arrange the meats, sauerkraut, and potatoes on a large platter. Discard the bay leaves. Serve with mustard, cornichons, and horseradish.

Pork Ribs Hunter's Style

Whether you call this dish *chasseur, cacciatora,* or hunter's style, you can expect it to include mushrooms, since a hunter would want to flavor his game with some wild mushrooms, such as chanterelles for extra flavor. This French version is delectable made with meaty pork ribs, but you can substitute chicken, lamb, or even rabbit or venison. Serve the ribs with Polenta with Sheep's-Milk Cheese and Crème Fraîche (page 184).

SERVES 6

3 pounds country pork ribs, cut into individual ribs

2 tablespoons olive oil

Salt and freshly ground pepper

2 medium onions, halved and thinly sliced

1 cup tomato puree

3 large garlic cloves, minced

2 tablespoons tomato paste

½ teaspoon herbes de Provence

Pinch of ground allspice

8–10 ounces white button mushrooms, halved or quartered

Chopped fresh flat-leaf parsley

Pat the ribs dry with paper towels.

In a large skillet, heat the oil over medium heat. Add as many of the ribs as will fit in the pan without touching. Cook them in batches, turning occasionally, until nicely browned on all sides, about 20 minutes total. Place the browned ribs in a large slow cooker. Sprinkle with salt and pepper to taste.

Spoon off all but 2 tablespoons of the fat from the skillet. Add the onions to the skillet and cook for 10 minutes, or until tender. Stir in the tomato puree, garlic, tomato paste, herbes de Provence, and allspice. Bring the sauce to a simmer, stirring well.

Scrape the contents of the skillet into the slow cooker. Cover and cook on low for 8 hours, or until the meat is tender and coming away from the bones.

When the ribs are almost ready, stir in the mushrooms. Cover and cook for 30 minutes more.

Discard any loose bones and skim off the fat. Sprinkle with parsley and serve hot.

Seafood

Seafood

Mussels in Fennel and Tomato Broth 121

Bouillabaisse 122

Slow-Cooked Salmon with Lemon and Green Olives 124

Salmon Steaks with Mustard and Parsley 126

Salmon with Tomatoes and Mint 127

Halibut with Maître d'Hôtel Butter 128

Basque Tuna and Potato Stew 129

Calamari Niçoise with Black Olives 131

Mussels in Fennel and Tomato Broth

Long, slow cooking produces a richly flavored broth for simmering mussels. Clams, shrimp, or chunks of firm white fish can be substituted for the mussels in this lively stew. A dash of anise-flavored liqueur is a nice finishing touch *à la française* but not essential.

SERVES 4

- 2 tablespoons olive oil
- 1 medium onion, thinly sliced
- 3 large garlic cloves, minced
- 1 teaspoon fennel seeds, crushed
- 1 cup dry white wine
- 1 cup bottled clam juice, Chicken Broth (page 40), or store-bought chicken broth
- 2 cups chopped peeled (see page 18) and seeded fresh tomatoes or chopped canned tomatoes
- Salt
- 2 pounds mussels, scrubbed and beards removed
- 2 tablespoons Pernod or other anise-flavored liqueur (optional)
- 2 tablespoons chopped fresh tarragon, basil, or flat-leaf parsley
- Toasted French bread for serving

In a small skillet, heat the oil over medium heat. Add the onion and cook, stirring often, until tender, about 10 minutes. Stir in the garlic and fennel seeds and cook for 1 minute more. Add the wine and bring to a simmer. Pour the mixture into a large slow cooker.

Add the clam juice, tomatoes, and a pinch of salt. Cover and cook on high for 3 to 4 hours.

Add the mussels and Pernod, if using. Cover and cook for 15 to 30 minutes more, or until the mussels are open.

Sprinkle with the herbs and serve hot with toasted French bread.

Bouillabaisse

Vegetables, wine, herbs, and clam juice simmer together as the base for this classic fish stew. In Marseille, seafood bouillabaisse is made with a variety of white fish and seafood. Be sure to serve it with rouille, a garlicky roasted red pepper mayonnaise that really lifts the flavor.

SERVES 6

- 2 cups chopped peeled (see page 18) and seeded fresh tomatoes or chopped canned tomatoes
- 3 medium carrots, peeled and chopped
- 2 celery ribs, chopped
- 1 large fennel bulb, chopped, green tops trimmed, with feathery leaves chopped and reserved
- 1 medium leek, trimmed, well washed, and sliced
- 3 tablespoons tomato paste
- 1 teaspoon herbes de Provence
- ¼ teaspoon piment d'Espelette (see page 18) or cayenne
- Pinch of saffron threads, crumbled
- Salt
- 4 cups water
- 1 cup dry white wine
- 1 cup bottled clam juice
- 1 pound boneless, skinless fish fillets, such as halibut, grouper, or monkfish
- 8 ounces sea scallops
- 8 ounces medium shrimp, peeled and deveined
- 1 baguette, cut into thin slices and toasted
- 6 small hardshell clams, soaked and scrubbed (optional)
- Rouille (page 218)

Combine the tomatoes, carrots, celery, fennel, and leek in a large slow cooker. Add the tomato paste, herbes de Provence, piment d'Espelette, saffron, and salt to taste. Add the water, wine, and clam juice. Cover and cook on high for 4 to 5 hours, or until the vegetables are tender.

Cut the fish, scallops, and shrimp into bite-size pieces and stir into the soup. Place the clams on top, if using. Cover and cook for 30 minutes more. Taste for seasoning.

Place a piece of bread in each soup dish. Add the bouillabaisse and sprinkle with the reserved fennel fronds. Serve hot with a spoonful of the rouille on top. Pass the remaining bread and rouille.

Slow-Cooked Salmon with Lemon and Green Olives

Mild green olives are a nice contrast, in both color and flavor, to the richness of salmon. The cooking time will depend on how thick the fish is and whether you prefer it rare or well done. To check for doneness, make a small slit in the thickest part of the salmon and peek inside. For rare, the fish should appear translucent; for well done, it will be opaque and flake easily. Serve this at room temperature on a bed of baby salad greens for a perfect summer meal.

SERVES 6

- 1 large lemon
- 2 medium shallots, thinly sliced
- ½ cup water
- 1 thick salmon fillet (about 2 pounds), cut into 6 pieces
- 2 tablespoons extra-virgin olive oil
   Salt and freshly ground pepper

SAUCE

- 2 tablespoons extra-virgin olive oil
- 1 tablespoon fresh lemon juice
- ½ teaspoon grated lemon zest
   Salt and freshly ground pepper
- ½ cup chopped pitted green olives
- 1 tablespoon chopped fresh flat-leaf parsley
- 1 tablespoon chopped rinsed capers

Thinly slice the lemon and remove the seeds. Scatter half of the shallots in a large slow cooker. Add half of the lemon slices and the water.

Rinse the salmon pieces and pat dry with paper towels. Rub the flesh side with the oil and sprinkle with salt and pepper to taste. Place the salmon skin side down in the slow cooker. Scatter the remaining lemon slices and shallots on top.

Cover and cook on low for 1 to 1½ hours, or until the salmon is cooked to taste. Check for doneness by making a small slit in the thickest part (see headnote).

MEANWHILE, MAKE THE SAUCE: In a small bowl, whisk the oil with the lemon juice, zest, and salt and pepper to taste. Add the olives, parsley, and capers.

With a large spatula, transfer the salmon, lemon, and shallots to dinner plates. Drizzle with the sauce and serve hot or at room temperature.

Salmon Steaks with Mustard and Parsley

Meaty fish like salmon do well in a slow cooker. Choose nice thick fillets or steaks so that they won't overcook. The salmon is coated with Dijon mustard and cooked on a bed of shallots. It's a simple preparation that's perfect for a weeknight meal.

SERVES 4 TO 8

- 1 tablespoon olive oil, plus more for the cooker
- 2 shallots, thickly sliced
- 3 tablespoons chopped fresh flat-leaf parsley
- 1½ tablespoons Dijon mustard
- 1 teaspoon fresh lemon juice
- 4 thick salmon steaks (about 2 pounds)
  Salt and freshly ground pepper

Oil a large slow cooker. Scatter the shallots in the slow cooker. In a small bowl, stir together the parsley, mustard, 1 tablespoon olive oil, and the lemon juice.

Sprinkle the salmon with salt and pepper to taste. Place the steaks side by side in the slow cooker. Spread the mustard mixture on top.

Cover and cook on high for 1 to 1½ hours, or until the salmon is done. It should be slightly translucent when a small slit is made in the center. Serve hot or at room temperature.

Salmon with Tomatoes and Mint

One summer my husband and I spent a few days in Eze, a tiny town perched on a hilltop in Provence. At a little bistro there, I had this beautiful dish made with a local Mediterranean fish. Now it is a favorite summer recipe. I make it with salmon in the slow cooker, where the gentle heat allows the fish to cook in its own juices and develop a delicate texture. I like the salmon just slightly rare in the center. Serve it with a chilled rosé.

SERVES 6

- 2 tablespoons olive oil, plus more for the cooker
- 2 cups halved cherry or grape tomatoes
- 1 cup torn fresh mint or basil leaves
- 1 thick salmon fillet (about 2 pounds), rinsed, patted dry, and cut into 6 pieces
  Salt and freshly ground pepper

Oil a large slow cooker. Add half of the tomatoes to the slow cooker in a single layer.

Sprinkle with half of the mint. Arrange the salmon skin side down over the mint. Drizzle with 2 tablespoons olive oil and sprinkle with salt and pepper to taste. Scatter the remaining mint over the salmon and top with the remaining tomatoes.

Cover and cook on low for 1 to 1½ hours, or until the salmon is done to taste. Check for doneness by making a small slit in the thickest part (see headnote on page 124). Serve hot or at room temperature.

Halibut with Maître d'Hôtel Butter

Maître d'hôtel butter is a compound butter made by mixing a few ingredients with softened butter. I usually make a double batch and keep it in the refrigerator or freezer, so that it's always at the ready to garnish steaks, fish, baked potatoes, noodles, and vegetables.

I like to use halibut steaks in this dish, but other thick, sturdy fish, such as salmon, are also good.

SERVES 4 TO 8

MAÎTRE D'HÔTEL BUTTER

4 tablespoons (½ stick) unsalted butter, softened

2 tablespoons chopped fresh flat-leaf parsley

½ teaspoon grated lemon zest

1 small garlic clove, minced

Salt and freshly ground pepper

Unsalted butter for the cooker

1 medium onion, sliced

4 halibut steaks, about 1 inch thick

Salt and freshly ground pepper

MAKE THE MAÎTRE D'HÔTEL BUTTER: In a small bowl, blend together the butter, parsley, lemon zest, garlic, and salt and pepper to taste. Form the mixture into a log, wrap it in plastic wrap, and refrigerate until ready to use.

Meanwhile, butter a large slow cooker. Scatter the onion slices in the cooker. Sprinkle the fish with salt and pepper to taste. Place the fish in the slow cooker. Cover and cook on high for 1 to 1½ hours, or until the fish is just slightly translucent when cut in the thickest part. Remove the fish with a slotted spatula.

Unwrap the butter log and cut it into thin slices. Place the butter on top of the fish and serve immediately.

Basque Tuna and Potato Stew

In the Basque language, this popular soup or stew is called *marmitako* (from the pot) because it is cooked in a casserole dish called a *marmita*. The slow cooker is a modern-day equivalent, cooking the vegetables into a flavorful base for the tuna. Note that the fish is added at the end of the cooking time so that it is not overdone.

If fresh tuna isn't available, use another firm-fleshed fish, such as swordfish. The potatoes should be very soft and falling apart.

SERVES 4

- 2 tablespoons olive oil
- 1 medium onion, chopped
- 1 red bell pepper, thinly sliced
- 1 green bell pepper, thinly sliced
- 2 garlic cloves, minced
- 1 teaspoon piment d'Espelette (see page 18) or paprika
  Salt
- 4 large russet (baking) potatoes (about 2 pounds), peeled and thinly sliced
- 1 cup halved cherry tomatoes
- ½ cup bottled clam juice or water
- 1 pound tuna or other firm-fleshed fish, cut into 1-inch cubes
  Freshly ground pepper

In a large skillet, heat the oil over medium heat. Add the onion and peppers and cook, stirring occasionally, for 10 minutes, or until the vegetables are softened. Stir in the garlic, piment d'Espelette, and salt to taste.

Place the potatoes in a large slow cooker. Add the sautéed vegetables, tomatoes, and clam juice and stir well. Cover and cook on low for 6 hours, or until the potatoes are very tender.

Sprinkle the tuna with salt and pepper to taste. Place the fish in the slow cooker, spooning some of the vegetables over the pieces. Cover and cook for 5 minutes, or until the tuna is just slightly pink in the center. Serve hot.

Calamari Niçoise with Black Olives

Calamari turn tender and sweet after long, slow cooking. Serve over pasta, hot rice, or couscous.

SERVES 6

- ¼ cup olive oil
- 2 medium onions, finely chopped
- 4 garlic cloves, finely chopped
- 1 cup dry white wine
- 3 cups chopped peeled (see page 18) and seeded fresh tomatoes, or one 28-ounce can tomatoes, drained and chopped
  Salt
- 3 pounds calamari, cleaned and cut into 1-inch rings
- ½ cup chopped imported pitted black olives
  Pinch of piment d'Espelette (see page 18) or crushed red pepper
  Chopped fresh basil

In a large heavy saucepan, heat the oil over medium heat. Add the onions and garlic and cook, stirring, until golden, about 10 minutes. Add the wine and bring to a simmer. Add the tomatoes and salt to taste. Bring to a simmer.

Pour the sauce into a large slow cooker. Stir in the calamari. Cover and cook on low for 2 hours, or until the calamari are tender.

Stir in the olives and piment d'Espelette. Cover and cook for 15 minutes more. Sprinkle with basil and serve hot.

Soufflés,
Quiches, and
Other Egg Dishes

Soufflés, Quiches, and Other Egg Dishes

Crustless Ham and Cheese Quiche 135

Fallen Cheese Soufflé 136

Goat Cheese and Walnut Soufflé 138

Spinach Soufflé 140

Crustless Vegetable Quiche 142

Tomato and Goat Cheese Flan 144

Bacon and Gruyère Pain Perdu 147

Mushroom Pain Perdu 149

Crustless Ham and Cheese Quiche

Custardy, delicate, and creamy, this quiche without a crust not only saves work but is also lower in calories than the traditional kind. Let it cool for a few minutes before cutting so that it firms up. It slices beautifully.

SERVES 6

    Unsalted butter
4 **ounces chopped ham**
8 **large eggs**
2 **tablespoons all-purpose flour**
    Pinch of freshly grated nutmeg
    Freshly ground pepper
1 **cup whole milk**
1 **cup heavy cream**
2 **cups grated Gruyère, Comté, or Emmental cheese**

Generously butter the insert of a large slow cooker. Scatter the ham in the slow cooker.

In a large bowl, beat the eggs with the flour, nutmeg, and pepper to taste until frothy. Beat in the milk and cream. Pour the egg mixture into the slow cooker. Scatter the cheese on top, avoiding the sides of the cooker.

Cover and cook on high for 2 hours and 15 minutes, or until the quiche is lightly puffed and a knife inserted near the center comes out clean.

Run a knife around the edge of the quiche. Cut into wedges and serve hot.

Fallen Cheese Soufflé

Don't worry about this soufflé collapsing. It's supposed to! It's made in much the same way as a standard soufflé, but instead of baking, it cooks in a steamy water bath in the slow cooker. When it is done, it sinks slightly and unmolds easily, like a beautiful savory cheesecake. Make this for a special brunch or lunch. It is particularly delicious drizzled with Tomato Sauce (page 221), or serve it with sautéed mushrooms, buttered peas, or spinach.

SERVES 4

- 2½ tablespoons unsalted butter, plus more for the dish
- ¾ cup freshly grated Parmigiano-Reggiano, Gruyère, or Emmental cheese
- 3 large egg yolks
- 6 large egg whites
- 3 tablespoons all-purpose flour
- ¾ cup whole milk, heated
- Pinch of freshly grated nutmeg
- Salt and freshly ground pepper

Generously butter a 6-cup soufflé dish. Sprinkle the dish with 2 tablespoons of the cheese.

Place the egg yolks in a large heatproof bowl. Place the egg whites in another large bowl.

In a small saucepan, melt the 2½ tablespoons butter over medium heat. Add the flour and stir with a wooden spoon to incorporate. Cook for 2 minutes, stirring constantly, until smooth and well blended. Remove from the heat. Gradually stir in the hot milk, nutmeg, and salt and pepper to taste. Return the saucepan to the heat and bring the mixture to a boil. Cook, stirring, for 2 minutes, or until thickened.

Gradually whisk the hot milk mixture into the egg yolks until blended. Don't add it all at once, or the yolks may scramble. Stir in the remaining cheese.

With an electric mixer, beat the egg whites with a pinch of salt on medium speed until frothy, about 30 seconds. Increase the speed to high and beat until soft peaks form, about 4 minutes.

With a rubber spatula, gently fold one quarter of the whites into the cheese mixture to lighten it. Fold in the remaining whites. Scrape the mixture into the prepared dish.

Place the dish on a rack in the insert of a large slow cooker (to improvise one, see page 9). Carefully pour hot water around the dish to a depth of 1 inch. Cover and cook on high for 1½ hours, or until the soufflé has risen and is set in the center.

Carefully remove the soufflé dish from the cooker. Run a knife around the inside of the dish. Invert a serving plate on top of the dish and quickly turn the dish over. Carefully remove the dish. Cut the soufflé into wedges and serve hot.

Goat Cheese and Walnut Soufflé

Slow cooker soufflés puff less dramatically than their oven-baked relatives, but they have all the flavor and delicate texture you expect from a soufflé. This version, made with toasted walnuts and goat cheese, is a favorite of mine for a speedy yet impressive lunch or appetizer. This soufflé isn't sturdy enough to unmold and is spooned directly from the casserole dish in which it cooks. All you need is a mixed salad of baby greens to accompany it.

SERVES 6

- 2½ tablespoons unsalted butter, plus more for the dish
- ½ cup chopped toasted walnuts
- 4 large eggs, separated
- ¼ cup all-purpose flour
- 1 cup whole milk, heated
- 1 teaspoon chopped fresh thyme
- Salt and freshly ground pepper
- 6 ounces fresh goat cheese, crumbled
- ¼ teaspoon cream of tartar

Generously butter a 6-cup soufflé dish. Sprinkle the dish with 1 tablespoon of the walnuts.

Place the egg yolks in a large heatproof bowl. Place the egg whites in another large bowl.

In a small saucepan, melt the 2½ tablespoons butter over medium heat. Add the flour and stir with a wooden spoon to incorporate. Cook for 2 minutes, stirring constantly, until smooth and well blended. Remove from the heat. Gradually stir in the hot milk, thyme, and salt and pepper to taste. Return the saucepan to the heat and bring the mixture to a boil. Cook, stirring, for 2 minutes, or until thickened.

Gradually whisk the hot milk mixture into the egg yolks until blended. Don't add it all at once, or the yolks may scramble. Stir in the cheese.

With an electric mixer, beat the egg whites with a pinch of salt on medium speed until frothy, about 30 seconds. Add the cream of tartar, increase the speed to high, and beat until the whites hold soft peaks, about 4 minutes. With a rubber spatula, gently fold one quarter of the whites into the cheese mixture to lighten it. Fold in the remaining whites. Fold in the remaining walnuts. Scrape the mixture into the prepared dish.

Place the dish on a rack in the insert of a large slow cooker (to improvise one, see page 9). Carefully pour hot water around the dish to a depth of 1 inch. Cover and cook on high for 1½ hours, or until the soufflé has risen and is softly set in the center. Carefully remove the soufflé dish from the cooker. Serve immediately, scooping the soufflé from the dish.

Spinach Soufflé

This soufflé does not rise much, but it has a nice airy texture and cheesy flavor. Serve it as a side dish with lamb chops.

SERVES 4

2½ tablespoons unsalted butter, plus more for the dish

¼ cup freshly grated Parmigiano-Reggiano

4 large eggs, separated

3 tablespoons all-purpose flour

1 cup whole milk, heated

¼ teaspoon freshly grated nutmeg

Salt and freshly ground pepper

¾ cup grated Comté or Gruyère cheese, lightly packed

1 10-ounce package frozen chopped spinach, thawed and squeezed dry

½ teaspoon cream of tartar

Generously butter a 6-cup soufflé dish. Sprinkle the dish with 2 tablespoons of the Parmesan.

Place the egg yolks in a large heatproof bowl. Place the egg whites in another large bowl.

In a small saucepan, melt the 2½ tablespoons butter over medium heat. Add the flour and stir with a wooden spoon to incorporate. Cook for 2 minutes, stirring constantly, until smooth and well blended. Remove from the heat. Gradually stir in the hot milk, nutmeg, ½ teaspoon salt, and pepper to taste. Return the saucepan to the heat and bring the mixture to a boil. Cook, stirring, for 2 minutes, or until thickened.

Gradually whisk the milk mixture into the egg yolks until blended. Don't add it all at once, or the yolks may scramble. Stir in the Comté cheese and the spinach.

With an electric mixer, beat the egg whites with a pinch of salt on medium speed until frothy, about 30 seconds. Add the cream of tartar and increase the speed to high. Beat until the whites hold soft peaks, about 4 minutes.

With a rubber spatula, gently fold one quarter of the whites into the spinach mixture to lighten it. Fold in the remaining whites. Scrape the mixture into the prepared dish. Sprinkle with the remaining Parmesan.

Place the dish on a rack in the insert of a large slow cooker (to improvise one, see page 9). Carefully pour hot water around the dish to a depth of 1 inch. Cover and cook on high for 1½ hours, or until the soufflé has risen and is just slightly jiggly in the center when the dish is tapped.

Carefully remove the soufflé dish from the cooker. Serve immediately, scooping the soufflé from the dish.

Crustless Vegetable Quiche

My first choice for this quiche is broccoli, but feel free to improvise with whatever vegetables you have on hand. Try asparagus, mushrooms, peppers, onions, or a mixture. You will need about 3 cups cooked vegetables.

SERVES 6

    Unsalted butter

6 **large eggs**

2 **tablespoons all-purpose flour**

½ **teaspoon salt**

⅛ **teaspoon freshly grated nutmeg**

    Freshly ground pepper

1 **cup half-and-half**

1 **cup whole milk**

3 **cups chopped well-drained cooked broccoli or other vegetables (see headnote)**

2 **tablespoons minced fresh tarragon or basil**

1 **cup grated Gruyère, Emmental, Gouda, or cheddar cheese (or a mixture)**

1 **cup freshly grated Parmigiano-Reggiano**

Generously butter a large slow cooker.

Beat the eggs with the flour, salt, nutmeg, and pepper to taste. Whisk in the half-and-half and milk. Stir in the broccoli, herbs, Gruyère, and ½ cup of the Parmesan.

Pour the mixture into the slow cooker. Sprinkle the remaining ½ cup Parmesan on top. Cover and cook on high for 1½ hours, or until the quiche is just set in the center. Run a knife around the edge of the quiche, cut into wedges, and serve hot.

Tomato and Goat Cheese Flan

With more egg per serving and less liquid than a quiche, this savory flan is similar, though its texture is a bit firmer. Serve it as a first course or as a lunch with a green bean salad.

SERVES 4

Unsalted butter

1 **cup halved cherry or grape tomatoes**

4 **ounces fresh goat cheese, crumbled**

1 **teaspoon chopped fresh thyme, basil, or chives**

6 **large eggs**

¼ **cup heavy cream**

¼ **cup whole milk**

Salt and freshly ground pepper

Generously butter a 6-cup soufflé dish. Place the tomatoes in the dish in a single layer. Scatter the goat cheese and herbs around the tomatoes.

In a medium bowl, whisk the eggs, cream, milk, and salt and pepper to taste. Pour the egg mixture over the tomatoes. Place a rack in the insert of a large slow cooker (to improvise one, see page 9). Place the soufflé dish on the rack. Carefully pour hot water around the dish to a depth of 1 inch. Cover and cook on high for 2 hours, or until just set and a knife inserted in the center comes out clean.

Carefully remove the dish from the cooker. Run a knife around the edge of the flan. Cut into wedges and serve hot or at room temperature.

Bacon and Gruyère
Pain Perdu

Guests staying overnight? In the morning, say *bonjour* with this delightful bread pudding known as *pain perdu*. It has all the flavors of a classic quiche Lorraine but is a lot less work.

You can assemble it in advance and let it sit for hours in the refrigerator if you like, so it is perfect for breakfast or brunch, or serve it with a green salad for an easy supper.

SERVES 6

    Unsalted butter
8 **ounces bacon**
2 **large shallots, finely chopped (about ½ cup)**
5 **large eggs**
2 **cups whole milk**
¼ **teaspoon freshly grated nutmeg**
    Salt and freshly ground pepper
1 **cup freshly grated Parmigiano-Reggiano**
6 **cups 1-inch-cubes day-old French bread**
½ **cup grated Gruyère or Emmental cheese**

Butter the insert of a large slow cooker.

In a large skillet, cook the bacon over medium heat until crisp and browned. Transfer to paper towels to drain. Crumble the bacon.

Pour off all but 1 tablespoon of the fat from the skillet. Add the shallots and cook over medium heat, stirring occasionally, until softened, about 2 minutes.

In a large bowl, beat the eggs until blended. Beat in the milk, nutmeg, and salt and pepper to taste. Stir in the bacon, shallots, and Parmesan. Place the bread cubes in a large bowl. Pour the mixture over the bread cubes and stir well.

Scrape the mixture into the slow cooker. Press the bread cubes down into the liquid. Sprinkle with the Gruyère.

Cover and cook on high for 1½ to 2 hours, or until a knife inserted in the center comes out clean. (It will take longer if it has been refrigerated overnight.) Serve hot, scooping it out of the dish.

Mushroom Pain Perdu

Lightly toasting the bread cubes gives this savory pudding a nice contrast of textures. The cubes on top stay crunchy, while those at the center become soft and creamy. Toasting is not essential, though, so if you don't have the time, just skip this step.

SERVES 6

- 3 tablespoons unsalted butter, plus more for the cooker
- 1 10-ounce package sliced mushrooms
- 1 small onion, finely chopped
- Salt and freshly ground pepper
- 5 large eggs
- 2 cups whole milk
- ½ cup freshly grated Parmigiano-Reggiano
- ¼ teaspoon freshly grated nutmeg
- 6 cups 1-inch-cubes day-old French bread, lightly toasted
- ½ cup grated Gruyère or Emmental cheese

Butter the insert of a large slow cooker.

In a large skillet, melt the 3 tablespoons butter over medium heat. Add the mushrooms and onion and cook, stirring often, until the mushroom juices evaporate and the mushrooms are golden, about 10 minutes. Season to taste with salt and pepper.

In a large bowl, beat the eggs until blended. Beat in the milk, Parmesan, nutmeg, ½ teaspoon salt, and pepper to taste. Stir in the mushrooms. Place the bread cubes in a large bowl. Pour the mixture over the bread cubes and stir well.

Scrape the mixture into the slow cooker. Press the bread cubes down into the liquid. Sprinkle with the Gruyère.

Cover and cook on high for 1½ to 2 hours, or until a knife inserted in the center comes out clean. Serve hot, scooping it out of the dish.

Vegetables

Vegetables

"Roasted" Beets with Butter and Herbs 153

"Roasted" Beet Salad with Roquefort and Walnuts 154

Braised Red Cabbage with Apples and Chestnuts 157

Cauliflower and Potatoes Catalan 158

New Potatoes with Butter and Herbs 159

French Potato Salad 160

Potato and Herb Gratin 162

Potatoes Pipérade.. 163

Potatoes Pissaladière 164

Butternut Squash Gratin 165

Summer Tian with Goat Cheese and Thyme 166

Vegetable Bouquet 167

"Roasted" Root Vegetables.. 168

Saffron Vegetable Stew... 169

"Roasted" Beets with Butter and Herbs

Beets are easy to prepare in the slow cooker. Without any added liquid, they come out sweet and tender, as though they had been oven-roasted. You can toss them with butter and chives or dill or use them for soups or salads.

SERVES 8 TO 10

- 6–8 medium red and/or golden beets, scrubbed
- 3 tablespoons unsalted butter
- 2 tablespoons chopped fresh chives or dill
- Salt and freshly ground pepper

Remove all but 1 inch of the beet tops. Leave the roots intact. Place the beets in a large slow cooker. Cover and cook on high for 3 to 4 hours, or until the beets are tender when pierced with a knife.

Let the beets cool slightly. With a small knife, peel off the skins. Serve hot tossed with the butter, herbs, and salt and pepper to taste.

Variation

Eliminate the butter and herbs. Chill the beets to use in salads.

"Roasted" Beet Salad with Roquefort and Walnuts

In France this would be called a composed salad because the ingredients are arranged on plates rather than being tossed. It makes a colorful and delicious appetizer, or serve it as a light meal with French bread.

SERVES 4 TO 6

    Vinaigrette (page 220)

2 **tablespoons chopped shallots or scallions**

6 **cups baby greens, washed and dried**

4 **roasted beets (see page 153), peeled and cut into ½-inch wedges**

4 **ounces Roquefort, Bleu d'Auvergne, or fresh goat cheese**

1 **cup walnut pieces, toasted**

Shake the vinaigrette with the shallots.

Just before serving, toss half of the dressing with the greens and arrange them on salad plates. Toss the remaining dressing with the beets. Spoon the beets over the greens. Crumble the cheese around the beets. Scatter the walnuts over all and serve.

Braised Red Cabbage with Apples and Chestnuts

Tangy, ruby-red cabbage studded with chestnuts goes with sausages, roast duck, pork chops, or turkey. Add some buttered egg noodles for a perfect winter meal.

Jarred or canned precooked chestnuts are good for this recipe. Just be sure they are unsweetened.

SERVES 8

- 1 head red cabbage (about 1½ pounds)
- 1 large apple, peeled and chopped
- ½ cup apple cider vinegar
- 2 tablespoons canola or vegetable oil
- 2 tablespoons sugar
- 1 bay leaf
- Salt and freshly ground pepper
- 2 cups peeled cooked chestnuts (see headnote)

Cut the cabbage into quarters and remove the hard core. Cut the wedges crosswise into thin shreds.

In a large slow cooker, combine the cabbage with the remaining ingredients except for the chestnuts, seasoning with salt and pepper to taste. Cover and cook on low for 5 to 6 hours, stirring occasionally, until the cabbage and apple are very tender.

Stir in the chestnuts, cover, and cook for 30 minutes more. Remove the bay leaf and serve hot.

Cauliflower and Potatoes Catalan

Sturdy vegetables like cauliflower and potatoes fare best in the slow cooker because they hold their shape and maintain their flavors. This simple combination is good with pot roast or stew. It is a classic recipe from the Catalan region of France, near Spain.

SERVES 8

- 1 pound Yukon Gold or other waxy potatoes, scrubbed and cut into 1-inch chunks
- 1 large cauliflower (about 1½ pounds), trimmed and cut into 1-inch florets
- ¼ cup olive oil
- 1 teaspoon salt
- Freshly ground pepper
- 1 cup Chicken Broth (page 40), store-bought chicken broth, vegetable broth, or water
- 2 tablespoons chopped fresh flat-leaf parsley, dill, or basil

Place the potatoes and cauliflower in a large slow cooker. Add the oil, salt, and pepper to taste and toss well. Add the broth. Cover and cook on high for 3 to 4 hours, or until tender.

Sprinkle with the herbs and taste for seasoning. Serve hot or at room temperature.

New Potatoes with Butter and Herbs

Potatoes turn out creamy, tender, and flavorful in the slow cooker. It is important that they are of equal size so that they cook evenly. If some are larger, halve or quarter them as needed.

SERVES 8

- 2 tablespoons unsalted butter, plus more for the cooker
- 2 pounds small new Yukon Gold or red potatoes, scrubbed
   Salt and freshly ground pepper
- ¼ cup chopped fresh flat-leaf parsley, chives, chervil, or dill
   (or a combination)

Butter the insert of a large slow cooker. Place the potatoes in the cooker and toss them with salt to taste. Cover and cook on high for 3 hours, or until they are tender when pierced with a knife.

Toss the potatoes with the 2 tablespoons butter and a generous grinding of pepper. Place them in a serving dish and top with the herbs. Serve hot.

French Potato Salad

Forgo the usual potato and mayo salad, and try this version instead. The dressing is a French-style vinaigrette boosted with a splash of white wine and fresh herbs. Cooking the potatoes in the slow cooker is an easy way to do a big batch without overcrowding them.

SERVES 8

Olive oil

3 pounds small Yukon Gold or other waxy potatoes

Salt

VINAIGRETTE

¼ cup finely chopped shallots or scallions

1 garlic clove, minced

1 teaspoon Dijon mustard

2 tablespoons fresh lemon juice

⅓ cup extra-virgin olive oil

¼ cup dry white wine or chicken broth

Salt and freshly ground pepper

2 tablespoons capers, rinsed and drained

2 tablespoons chopped fresh basil

2 tablespoons chopped fresh flat-leaf parsley

Oil the insert of a large slow cooker. Place the potatoes in the slow cooker and toss with salt to taste. Cover and cook on high for 3 hours, or until the potatoes are tender when pierced with a knife.

TO MAKE THE VINAIGRETTE: Place the shallots, garlic, mustard, lemon juice, oil, and wine in a covered jar. Season with salt and pepper to taste and shake well.

Remove the potatoes from the slow cooker and cut into 1-inch pieces. Add the capers and dressing and toss well. Sprinkle with the herbs and toss again. Serve warm or lightly chilled.

Potato and Herb Gratin

As a young bride, I picked up a copy of the great chef James Beard's book *Menus for Entertaining* and discovered this recipe. Of course, Mr. Beard baked his gratin in a conventional oven, but I find it works well in a slow cooker, especially when the oven is taken up with a roast.

SERVES 8

- 3 pounds russet (baking) potatoes, peeled and thinly sliced
- 2 garlic cloves, chopped
- 2 tablespoons chopped fresh flat-leaf parsley
- 1 tablespoon chopped fresh chives
- 1 teaspoon chopped fresh thyme
- ½ teaspoon salt
- Freshly ground pepper
- 3 tablespoons olive oil
- ½ cup water
- ½ cup grated cheese, such as Gruyère, Emmental, or Parmigiano-Reggiano

Place the potatoes in a large slow cooker. Sprinkle with the garlic, herbs, salt, and pepper to taste. Pour on the oil and water. Toss well.

Cover and cook on high for 6 hours, or until the potatoes are tender when pierced with a knife. Sprinkle with the cheese, cover, and cook for 10 minutes more, or until the cheese is melted. Let rest for 10 minutes before serving.

Potatoes Pipérade

Pipérade is a sauce of bell peppers, tomatoes, onions, and ham. In the Basque region, it is eaten with everything from eggs to fish, and it tastes great with potatoes too. Serve as a saucy accompaniment to an omelet or a roast chicken.

SERVES 8

Olive oil

Pipérade (page 222)

6 medium russet (baking) potatoes, peeled and sliced

Salt

Oil the insert of a large slow cooker. Spoon about one third of the pipérade into the bottom of the slow cooker. Arrange half of the potatoes on top. Sprinkle the potatoes with salt to taste. Make a second layer with one third of the sauce, the remaining potatoes, and salt to taste. Spoon the remaining sauce over the top.

Cover and cook on high for 6 hours, or until the potatoes are tender. Serve hot.

Potatoes Pissaladière

Pissaladière is a Provençal version of pizza. I've incorporated its typical toppings of onions, tomatoes, olives, and anchovies into a potato gratin with excellent results. Serve as a side dish or as a main course with a green salad.

SERVES 6 TO 8

¼ cup olive oil, plus more for the cooker

3 large onions, thinly sliced

Salt and freshly ground pepper

1 28-ounce can tomatoes, chopped

2 teaspoons chopped fresh rosemary or 1 teaspoon herbes de Provence

1 2-ounce can anchovy fillets

3 pounds russet (baking) potatoes, peeled and thinly sliced

¼ cup chopped pitted black olives, such as niçoise

Oil the insert of a large slow cooker. In a large skillet, heat the ¼ cup oil over medium-low heat. Add the onions and salt and pepper to taste and cook, stirring occasionally, until golden and very tender, about 10 minutes.

Drain the tomatoes and add them to the skillet with the rosemary. Cook for 10 minutes, or until thickened.

Drain the anchovies and reserve the oil. Chop the anchovies and stir them into the sauce.

Arrange half of the potatoes in the slow cooker and sprinkle with salt and pepper to taste. Spoon half of the sauce on top. Make a second layer with the remaining potatoes and sprinkle with salt and pepper to taste. Spread on the remaining sauce. Drizzle with the anchovy oil.

Cover and cook on high for 6 hours, or until the potatoes are very tender. Sprinkle with the olives. Serve hot or at room temperature.

Butternut Squash Gratin

You will want to serve this easy and colorful layered squash, potato, and cheese gratin all fall and winter alongside roasts and stews. Any hard winter squash can be used in this recipe. Hubbard, acorn, and delicata squash are good substitutes for the butternut.

SERVES 6 TO 8

3 tablespoons unsalted butter, plus more for the cooker
2 pounds russet (baking) potatoes, peeled and thinly sliced
1 pound butternut squash, peeled and thinly sliced
  Salt and freshly ground pepper
1 cup freshly grated Parmigiano-Reggiano or Emmental cheese
½ cup chicken broth

Butter the insert of a large slow cooker. Scatter about one third of the potatoes and squash in the cooker. Season with salt and pepper to taste. Sprinkle with ⅓ cup of the cheese and dot with 1 tablespoon of the butter. Add the broth.

Repeat with 2 more layers, reserving the final ⅓ cup cheese. Cover and cook on low for 6 hours, or until the vegetables are tender when pierced with a knife. Sprinkle with the reserved cheese. Cover and cook for 10 minutes more. Serve hot.

Summer Tian with Goat Cheese and Thyme

A *tian* is a Provençal dish, usually composed of vegetables baked in a shallow casserole, often with cheese. In the heat of summer, I cook this colorful version early in the day and then serve it at room temperature with bread for a light lunch.

SERVES 4 TO 6

 3 tablespoons olive oil, plus more for the cooker

 2 large red onions, sliced

 1 pound Yukon Gold or red potatoes, scrubbed and sliced about ¼ inch thick

 1½ pounds green and yellow zucchini, sliced about ¼ inch thick

 1 pound plum tomatoes, sliced about ¼ inch thick

 1 tablespoon chopped fresh thyme

 Salt and freshly ground pepper

 4 ounces fresh goat cheese, crumbled

Oil the insert of a large slow cooker. Make a layer of one third of the onions, potatoes, zucchini, and tomatoes. Sprinkle with 1 teaspoon of the thyme and salt and pepper to taste. Drizzle with 1 tablespoon of the oil. Make 2 more layers in the same way. Cover and cook on high for 4 hours, or until the potatoes are tender.

Uncover and sprinkle with the cheese. Cover and cook for 15 minutes more, or until the cheese is melted. Serve warm or at room temperature.

Vegetable Bouquet

Here is the perfect side dish for roast leg of lamb or chicken, a simple combination of tender potatoes and spring vegetables. Cook the vegetables just until the potatoes are creamy and the carrots still have a nice snap.

SERVES 8

- 1½ pounds small new potatoes, such as Yukon Gold
- 2 cups baby carrots
- 1 10-ounce package frozen artichoke hearts, partially thawed
- 1 cup frozen pearl onions, partially thawed
  Salt and freshly ground pepper
- ½ cup chicken or vegetable broth
- 1 10-ounce package frozen petite peas, partially thawed
- 3 tablespoons cold unsalted butter
- 2 tablespoons chopped fresh flat-leaf parsley, chives, or basil (optional)

Scrub the potatoes and place them in a large slow cooker. Add the carrots, artichoke hearts, and onions. Sprinkle with salt and pepper to taste and pour over the broth. Cover and cook on high for 2½ to 3 hours, or until the potatoes are tender.

Add the peas, cover, and cook for 10 minutes more to heat them through. Cut the butter into thin slices and place them over the top. Sprinkle with the herbs, if using. Season to taste with salt and pepper and stir gently. Serve hot.

"Roasted" Root Vegetables

I make this dish a lot in wintertime, when green vegetables are scarce. You can also add some less typical but very French vegetables, like rutabaga, parsnips, or celeriac. The slow cooker not only tenderizes firm vegetables as they cook but also mellows and sweetens their flavor.

SERVES 8

- 1½ pounds new potatoes, such as Yukon Gold, peeled and cut into 1-inch pieces
- 1½ pounds turnips, peeled and cut into 1-inch pieces
- 4 large carrots, peeled and cut into 1-inch pieces
- 6 shallots, sliced
- 10 garlic cloves, peeled
- 4 tablespoons (½ stick) unsalted butter
- Salt and freshly ground pepper
- 2 tablespoons finely chopped fresh flat-leaf parsley

In a large slow cooker, combine all the ingredients except for the parsley, seasoning with salt and pepper to taste.

Stir well. Cover and cook on high for 3½ to 4 hours, or until all the vegetables are tender.

Serve hot, sprinkled with the parsley.

Saffron Vegetable Stew

A vegetable stew is just the thing when you want something light yet satisfying. And, of course, it is perfect for vegetarians. This Provençal combination marries cauliflower, potatoes, and onions with tomatoes and saffron. I serve it as a main course over couscous or rice or as a side dish with grilled fish or pork chops. To me, it tastes best when it is just warm or at room temperature. It keeps well and is good the next day too.

SERVES 6 TO 8

- 2 tablespoons olive oil
- 2 medium onions, chopped
- 2 garlic cloves, chopped
- 2 cups chopped canned tomatoes with their juice
- 2 teaspoons salt
- ¼ teaspoon saffron threads, crumbled
  Freshly ground pepper
- 4 medium boiling potatoes, such as Yukon Gold, peeled and cut into 1-inch chunks
- 1 medium cauliflower, trimmed and cut into florets
- 1–2 teaspoons chopped fresh thyme or basil

In a large skillet, heat the oil over medium heat. Add the onions and cook, stirring occasionally, until golden but not browned, about 10 minutes. Stir in the garlic and cook for 1 minute more. Add the tomatoes and their juices, salt, saffron, and pepper to taste. Bring to a simmer and cook for 5 minutes, or until thickened.

Put the potatoes in a large slow cooker. Place the cauliflower over the potatoes. Pour the tomato sauce over all.

Cover and cook on high for 3 hours, or until the vegetables are tender when pierced with a knife. Serve hot, sprinkled with the thyme.

Legumes and Grains

Legumes and
Grains

Basic Lentils 173

Warm Lentil Salad with Bacon and Vinaigrette 174

Beans à la Française 175

Beans Bretonne 176

Warm Bean Salad with Mustard Vinaigrette 177

Creamy White Bean Brandade 179

Moroccan Vegetable Couscous 180

Polenta with Ham, Cheese, and Tomato Sauce 182

Polenta with Sheep's-Milk Cheese and Crème Fraîche 184

Rice Pilaf 185

Rice Pilaf with Golden Raisins and Pistachios 186

Spelt Pilaf with Mushrooms... 187

Basic Lentils

Serve these lentils straight from the slow cooker, or use them in one of the recipes that follow.

MAKES 6 CUPS LENTILS; SERVES 8

- 1 pound brown lentils, rinsed and picked over
- 6 cups water
- 2 whole cloves
- 1 medium onion, peeled
- 1 bay leaf
- Salt

Put the lentils in a large slow cooker and add the water. Stick the cloves in the onion and add it to the lentils with the bay leaf. Cover and cook on high for 4 to 5 hours, or until the lentils are tender. Add salt to taste. Let stand for 10 minutes.

Discard the onion and bay leaf. Drain the lentils and serve hot.

Variation

For Lentils with Scallions, toss the cooked lentils with 3 tablespoons unsalted butter, ¼ cup finely chopped scallions, and salt and pepper to taste.

OUT OF THE POT *Warm Lentil Salad with Bacon and Vinaigrette*

The lentils absorb the flavors better if they are warm when you add the dressing, so if you have cooked the lentils in advance, reheat them before tossing. Serve this salad with grilled knockwurst and coleslaw.

SERVES 8

Basic Lentils (page 173), drained (see headnote)
Vinaigrette (page 220)
¼ cup minced shallots or scallions
Salt and freshly ground pepper
¼ cup chopped fresh flat-leaf parsley
4 ounces bacon, cooked crisp, drained, and chopped

In a large serving bowl, stir together the lentils, vinaigrette, and shallots. Season with salt and pepper to taste.

Stir in the parsley and bacon and serve warm.

Beans à la Française

Pale green flageolets are a favorite French bean variety, as are small, round white beans and the large, flat Tarbais beans, but any kind of beans, including Great Northern, cannellini, kidney, pea beans, or chickpeas, can be cooked this way.

These beans are a good side dish sprinkled with freshly ground pepper and drizzled with extra-virgin olive oil or tossed with some butter.

MAKES 6 CUPS

- 1 pound flageolet, cannellini, Great Northern, or other beans, rinsed and picked over
- 1 large carrot, peeled and halved
- 1 celery rib, halved
- 1 medium onion, peeled
- 1 garlic clove, peeled
- 2 fresh flat-leaf parsley sprigs
- 2 teaspoons salt

Place the beans in a large bowl with cold water to cover by several inches. Soak in a cool place for 6 hours or overnight. Drain the beans.

Place the beans in a large slow cooker. Add the vegetables, garlic, parsley, and salt. Add fresh water to cover by 1 inch.

Cover and cook on high for 4 to 6 hours, or until completely tender. (Taste a few beans to be sure.) Discard the vegetables. Serve the beans hot as a side dish or use them in salads, soups, or stews.

OUT OF THE POT *Beans Bretonne*

Once you have cooked dried beans, there are so many ways to use them. Here is one of my favorites. It goes well with grilled sliced steak, or serve over rice or noodles.

SERVES 4 TO 6

1 medium onion, finely chopped

1 large garlic clove, minced

3 tablespoons unsalted butter

1 cup chopped peeled (see page 18) and seeded fresh tomatoes or chopped canned tomatoes

½ cup dry white wine

3 cups Beans à la Française (page 175), drained

Salt and freshly ground pepper

In a medium saucepan over medium heat, cook the onion and garlic in the butter until tender, about 8 minutes. Add the tomatoes and wine and bring the sauce to a simmer. Cook for 10 minutes, or until slightly thickened.

Stir in the beans and salt and pepper to taste. Simmer for 5 minutes, or until heated through. Serve hot.

OUT OF THE POT *Warm Bean Salad with Mustard Vinaigrette*

In the summer, I like to serve these beans as part of a Niçoise-type salad with hard-cooked eggs, canned tuna, and sliced tomatoes on a bed of salad greens. They are also good with grilled sausages or fish steaks.

SERVES 4 TO 6

3	cups Beans à la Française (page 175), drained
	Vinaigrette (page 220)
1½	tablespoons Dijon mustard
½	cup chopped scallions
2	teaspoons chopped fresh herbs, such as flat-leaf parsley, chives, or basil
	Salt and freshly ground pepper

If the beans are cold, warm them gently. Drain off any excess liquid.

In a large serving bowl, whisk together the vinaigrette and mustard. Add the beans and toss gently. Stir in the scallions and herbs and toss again. Season with salt and pepper to taste. Serve warm.

OUT OF THE POT *Creamy White Bean Brandade*

A classic *brandade* is made with poached salt cod whipped to a fine puree. Served as an appetizer, it is spread on toasted French bread. This easy bean version is a delightful variation that can be put together in no time.

Serve it as an appetizer with raw vegetables, crackers, or toasted French bread. It also makes a good side dish with grilled steak, tuna, or swordfish.

SERVES 6

- 3 cups Beans à la Française (page 175), drained
- 6 anchovy fillets, drained
- 2 teaspoons chopped fresh rosemary
- 1 garlic clove, peeled
- ¼ cup extra-virgin olive oil
- 2 tablespoons fresh lemon juice
- Salt and freshly ground pepper

Place the beans, anchovies, rosemary, and garlic in a food processor. Puree until smooth. Blend in the olive oil and lemon juice. Season with salt and pepper to taste. Serve at room temperature or lightly chilled.

Moroccan Vegetable Couscous

In the nineteenth and twentieth centuries, France colonized Morocco, Algeria, and Tunisia in North Africa, and the French who settled there acquired a taste for the spicy local cooking. The countries became independent in the 1950s and 1960s, and many French people returned to France, followed by many Africans seeking work. Today, restaurants that feature the flavors of North Africa are common throughout France. Couscous is considered a national dish, and you will find it everywhere from the local *traiteur,* or take-out shop, to school cafeterias.

Although the ingredients list is long, this vegetarian version is actually a very simple recipe. For a *couscous royal*, top with grilled Merguez sausages, chicken, or lamb kebabs before serving.

SERVES 6

- 4 medium Yukon Gold or red potatoes, cut into wedges
- 1 small cauliflower, cut into 1-inch pieces
- 4 large carrots, peeled and quartered
- 2 large onions, quartered
- 2 cups cooked or canned chickpeas, drained
- 10 cups water
- 3 tablespoons olive oil
- 2 garlic cloves, minced
- 2 tablespoons ground turmeric
- 1 teaspoon ground cinnamon
- 1 teaspoon ground coriander
- Pinch of saffron threads, crumbled
- 1 teaspoon salt
- 1 teaspoon harissa or hot sauce, plus more for serving

COUSCOUS

- 2 cups couscous
- 3 cups Chicken Broth (page 40), store-bought chicken broth, vegetable broth, or water
- 2 tablespoons unsalted butter
- Salt
- ¼ cup chopped fresh cilantro

Combine the vegetables, chickpeas, water, oil, garlic, spices, salt, and harissa in a large slow cooker. Cover and cook on low for 8 hours, or until the vegetables are tender.

When the vegetables are almost ready, place the couscous in a large heatproof bowl. Heat the broth to boiling with the butter and salt to taste. Pour the broth over the couscous and let stand for 5 minutes, or until the couscous is tender and the liquid is absorbed.

To serve, pile the couscous onto a platter. Spoon some of the vegetables and broth on top. Sprinkle with the cilantro. Pass the remaining vegetables and broth at the table, accompanied by harissa.

Polenta with Ham, Cheese, and Tomato Sauce

The gentle, steady heat of the slow cooker is perfect for cooking polenta. For a special brunch, serve with fried eggs and asparagus or peas.

SERVES 8

- 2 cups coarsely ground yellow cornmeal, preferably stone-ground
- 1 teaspoon salt
- 4 cups Chicken Broth (page 40) or store-bought chicken broth
- 4 cups water
- 8 ounces ham, cut into small dice
- 4 ounces Gruyère or Emmental cheese, grated
- 3 tablespoons unsalted butter
  Tomato Sauce (page 221)

Stir together the cornmeal, salt, broth, and water in a large slow cooker. Cover and cook on high for 2 hours. Stir well. Cover and cook for 30 to 60 minutes more, or until the polenta is thickened. If it seems too thick, stir in a little warm water.

Spoon the polenta into a serving dish. Stir in the ham, cheese, and butter. Serve hot with the tomato sauce.

Polenta with Sheep's-Milk Cheese and Crème Fraîche

In the French Alps of the Haute-Savoie region, polenta is lavishly mixed with cheese and cream, the perfect food for a cold winter night or *après-ski*. Use a young sheep's-milk cheese for this, one that is flavorful but not too sharp.

SERVES 8

- 1½ cups coarsely ground yellow cornmeal, preferably stone-ground
- 1 teaspoon salt
- 4 cups water
- 3 cups Chicken Broth (page 40), store-bought chicken broth, or vegetable broth
- 8 ounces French brébis or other sheep's-milk cheese
- 4 ounces crème fraîche (see page 14) or sour cream

Stir together the cornmeal, salt, water, and broth in a large slow cooker. Cover and cook on high for 2 hours. Stir well. Cover and cook for 30 to 60 minutes more, or until the polenta is thickened. If it seems too thick, stir in a little warm water.

Turn off the heat. Stir in the cheese and crème fraîche. Taste for seasoning. Serve hot.

Rice Pilaf

Here's a convenient way to make a batch of rice that leaves you free to do other things as it cooks unattended. Use converted rice, which holds its shape and texture in the slow cooker.

SERVES 8

- 1 small onion, finely chopped
- 3 cups converted rice
- 3 cups Chicken Broth (page 40) or store-bought chicken broth
- 3 cups water
- Salt
- 2 tablespoons unsalted butter

Place the onion and rice in a large slow cooker. Stir in the broth, water, and salt to taste. Cover and cook on high for 1½ to 2 hours, or until the rice is tender.

Add the butter and stir well. Serve hot.

Rice Pilaf with Golden Raisins and Pistachios

Flecked with golden raisins and green pistachios, this lovely pilaf is good with seafood or pork. Try it with other dried fruits and nuts too, such as apricots and almonds or cranberries and walnuts. Use converted rice, which holds its shape and texture in the slow cooker.

SERVES 8 TO 10

- 3 cups Chicken Broth (page 40) or store-bought chicken broth
- 3 cups water
- Salt
- 3 cups converted rice
- 1 2-inch sprig fresh rosemary or 2 fresh thyme sprigs
- 3 tablespoons unsalted butter
- ¼ cup minced shallots
- ½ cup chopped shelled pistachios
- ½ cup golden raisins

Combine the broth, water, and salt to taste in a large slow cooker. Add the rice and rosemary and stir well. Cover and cook on high for 1½ to 2 hours, or until the rice is tender.

Discard the rosemary. Stir in the butter, shallots, pistachios, and raisins. Serve hot.

Spelt Pilaf with Mushrooms

Spelt has become very popular in France over the past decade or two. It is similar to wheat or farro, with a nutty flavor and chewy texture. Use it in soup, or cook it in a pilaf like this one. You can find it at most health food stores.

SERVES 8 TO 10

- 3 cups spelt, farro, or wheat berries (see headnote)
- 8 ounces sliced white button mushrooms
- ½ cup finely chopped shallots
- 6 cups Classic French Beef Broth (page 41) or store-bought beef broth
  Salt and freshly ground pepper
- ½ cup heavy cream
- ½ cup freshly grated Parmigiano-Reggiano

Combine the spelt, mushrooms, shallots, broth, and salt and pepper to taste in a large slow cooker. Cover and cook on high for 2 hours, or until the spelt is tender and the liquid is absorbed.

Uncover and stir in the cream and Parmesan. Taste for seasoning. Serve hot.

Desserts

Desserts

Tea-Spiced Pears 191

Honeyed Pears with Goat Cheese and Thyme 193

Lemon Pots de Crème 194

Bittersweet Chocolate Creams 197

Bistro Crème Caramel 198

Ginger Crème Brûlée 200

Peach Flan 202

Creamy Cherry Clafoutis 203

Raspberry Brioche Pudding 204

Apricot French Bread Pudding 206

Rice Pudding 207

Prune Custard Cake 208

Orange Soufflé 209

Queen of Sheba Cake (Reine de Saba) 210

Corsican Honey Cheesecake 213

Chocolate Pain Perdu (Chocolate Bread Pudding) 214

Tea-Spiced Pears

In this recipe, pears are poached in a syrup made with wine, sugar, spices, and Earl Grey tea. They make a perfect light finish to a rich meal.

Earl Grey tea is known for its distinctive floral flavor and aroma of bergamot, a variety of orange that has the color of a lemon. The tea was named for a nineteenth-century British prime minister who received the recipe as a diplomatic gift. He gave it to a tea company, which still produces it today.

SERVES 8

- 2 Earl Grey tea bags
- 1 cup boiling water
- 1 cup dry white wine
- ¾ cup sugar
- 1 2-inch strip orange zest
- 4 whole cloves
- 2 whole star anise
- 8 Bosc, Bartlett, or Anjou pears
  Crème fraîche (see page 14) or whipped cream

Place the tea bags in the boiling water and let stand for 3 minutes. Remove the tea bags and pour the tea into a large slow cooker. Add the wine, sugar, orange zest, cloves, and star anise and stir well.

Wash the pears and place them standing upright in the slow cooker. Cover and cook on low for 4 hours, or until the pears are tender when pierced with a knife.

Remove the pears from the syrup. Strain the syrup over the pears. Let cool slightly, then cover and refrigerate.

Serve chilled with a dollop of crème fraîche.

Honeyed Pears with Goat Cheese and Thyme

Pears cooked with honey and lemon are a light and sophisticated dessert, wonderful with goat cheese and a sprinkling of fresh thyme. They are equally good for breakfast with yogurt and granola.

SERVES 8

- 8 Bosc, Bartlett, or Anjou pears
- 1 lemon
- ½ cup water
- ½ cup honey
- 4 ounces fresh goat cheese, sliced
  Fresh thyme sprigs

Wash the pears and place them standing upright in a large slow cooker.

Peel off a 2-inch strip of lemon zest. Squeeze the lemon to get 2 tablespoons juice.

In a measuring cup, combine the water, honey, and lemon juice and stir well. Pour the liquid over the pears. Add the zest.

Cover and cook on low for 4 hours or on high for 2 hours, or until the pears are tender when pierced with a knife.

Carefully remove the pears from the cooker and pour the juices over all. Cover and chill until serving time.

Place a pear on each serving plate. Add a slice or two of goat cheese and garnish with a few thyme sprigs.

Lemon Pots de Crème

Smooth and delicate, these silky lemon custards are especially good after a fish dinner.

Adding hot water to the slow cooker helps to distribute the heat to ensure that the puddings cook evenly. Just be careful not to splash the water into the cups, and be sure to protect your hands with rubber gloves when you remove the cups from the cooker so that you don't burn your fingertips.

Too delicate to be unmolded, these creams are served in the cups in which they are cooked, perhaps with a crisp butter or almond cookie on the side.

SERVES 4

⅓ cup fresh lemon juice

½ teaspoon grated lemon zest

½ cup sugar

4 large egg yolks

1 cup heavy cream

Stir together the lemon juice, zest, and sugar until the sugar is dissolved.

In a large bowl, whisk the egg yolks and cream until blended. Stir in the lemon juice mixture.

Scrape the mixture into four ½-cup custard cups or ramekins. Place a rack in the insert of a large slow cooker (to improvise one, see page 9). Carefully place the cups on the rack. Pour about 1 inch of hot water into the cooker. Cover and cook on high for 2 hours, or until the creams are softly set and slightly jiggly in the center. Uncover and let stand for 10 minutes. Carefully remove the cups from the cooker (see headnote).

Cover and refrigerate until chilled, 2 hours, or up to 3 days, before serving.

Bittersweet Chocolate Creams

The gentle heat of the slow cooker is perfect for melting the chocolate and softly cooking the eggs for these rich and intensely chocolaty creams. A small amount goes a long way, so I sometimes serve these in demitasse cups with tiny coffee spoons, either plain or decorated with a dollop of whipped cream and some chocolate shavings or a chocolate-covered espresso bean. If you don't have an espresso maker, espresso made from instant powder is fine, or substitute strong brewed coffee.

SERVES 8

- 2 tablespoons sugar
- 3 large eggs
- 2 cups heavy cream
- ¼ cup espresso or strong coffee
- 8 ounces bittersweet (not unsweetened) chocolate, broken into small pieces
- 1 teaspoon vanilla extract
- Chocolate-covered coffee beans (optional)
- Whipped cream (optional)

In a heatproof bowl that will fit in the slow cooker, beat together the sugar, eggs, cream, and espresso until blended and the sugar is dissolved. Add the chocolate and stir well.

Place a rack in the insert of a large slow cooker (to improvise one, see page 9). Place the bowl on the rack. Pour hot water around the bowl to a depth of 1 inch. Cover and cook on high for 1½ hours, or until the chocolate is melted and the surface appears foamy.

Carefully remove the bowl from the cooker. Whisk the mixture until blended. Add the vanilla. Spoon the mixture into eight ramekins or demitasse cups.

Cover and refrigerate until well chilled and serve plain or garnished with the coffee beans and/or whipped cream.

Bistro Crème Caramel

A French classic, crème caramel is one of the simplest desserts. Made with evaporated milk and sweetened condensed milk, this version is the best I have ever tried—and I have tried quite a few! I keep the canned ingredients in the pantry so that I can serve it any time.

To chill it quickly and serve it sooner, place the dish in a shallow bowl filled with ice and water.

SERVES 8

- 1 cup sugar
- ¼ cup water
- 1 12-ounce can evaporated whole milk
- 1 14-ounce can sweetened condensed milk
- 4 large eggs
- 1 teaspoon vanilla extract

Combine the sugar and water in a small saucepan. Cook over medium heat, swirling the pan occasionally, until the sugar is dissolved. Simmer the mixture without stirring until it begins to turn brown. Gently swirl the pan until the syrup is evenly caramelized.

Protect your hand with an oven mitt and pour the hot syrup into a 6-cup soufflé dish, turning the dish to coat the bottom evenly. Let cool until the caramel is just set.

Whisk together the evaporated and condensed milks in a large bowl. Beat in the eggs and vanilla until blended. Pour the mixture into the soufflé dish.

Place a rack in the insert of a large slow cooker (to improvise one, see page 9). Place the dish on the rack. Pour hot water around the dish to a depth of 1 inch. Cover and cook on high for 2 to 2½ hours, or until a knife inserted near the center comes out clean.

Carefully remove the dish from the slow cooker. Let cool slightly, then cover and refrigerate until chilled, several hours or overnight.

To serve, run a knife around the inside of the dish. Invert a serving plate on top of the dish and quickly turn the dish over. Carefully remove the dish, allowing the caramel to drizzle over the custard. Cut into wedges and serve.

Ginger Crème Brûlée

A hint of fresh ginger adds an intriguing flavor to this simple but very elegant dessert. The creamy, rich custard is covered with a caramelized sugar topping. Kitchenware stores sell small blowtorches that you can use to make the crunchy topping, but popping the ramekins under the broiler works just fine.

SERVES 4

- 2 cups heavy cream
- ½ cup plus 4 tablespoons sugar
- 2–3 tablespoons grated fresh ginger
- 5 large egg yolks
- 1 teaspoon vanilla extract

Heat the cream in a medium saucepan over medium heat until small bubbles appear around the edge. Remove from the heat. Add the ½ cup sugar and the ginger. Stir until the sugar dissolves.

In a medium bowl, whisk the egg yolks until blended. Slowly beat in the cream mixture and the vanilla. Pour the cream through a fine sieve into four 6-ounce ramekins.

Place a rack in the insert of a large slow cooker (to improvise one, see page 9). Place the ramekins on the rack. Carefully pour hot water around the ramekins to a depth of 1 inch. Cover and cook on high for 2 hours, or until the custard is set but slightly jiggly in the center.

Uncover and turn off the heat. Leave the ramekins in the cooker until they are cool enough to handle. Remove the ramekins. Cover and chill for several hours or overnight.

Just before serving, blot any moisture from the surface of the custards with a paper towel. Place an oven rack about 3 inches from the broiler and turn the broiler to high. Place the cups on a baking sheet. Sprinkle the surface of each custard with 1 tablespoon of the remaining sugar. Place under the broiler for 2 to 3 minutes, or until browned and bubbling. Watch them carefully so that they do not burn.

Remove the custards from the oven and let cool for 5 minutes before serving.

Variation

For Vanilla Crème Brûlée, omit the fresh ginger.

Peach Flan

One winter day, I wanted to try this flan using frozen peaches, but when I got to the market, there were none in the freezer and there were no fresh peaches available. Then I remembered something I had read in Dorie Greenspan's *Baking: From My Home to Yours*: many French cooks use canned pears when baking fruit tarts. I decided to apply the same idea to the flan and bought some canned peaches. The result was a success. So convenient! No peeling or pitting. Peaches are my favorite, but other fruits, such as pears, cherries, or plums, also work in this recipe.

SERVES 4 TO 6

 1 **30-ounce can sliced peaches in heavy syrup, drained (about 3 cups), or substitute peeled and sliced fresh or thawed frozen peaches**
    Unsalted butter
 ½ **cup sugar**
 2 **large eggs**
 ½ **cup heavy cream**
 ¼ **cup whole milk**
 1–2 **drops almond extract**

Blot the peach slices dry with paper towels. Generously butter the bottom and 2 inches up the sides of the insert of a large slow cooker. Sprinkle the bottom with 2 tablespoons of the sugar. Arrange the peach slices in the cooker in a single layer.

Whisk the eggs, cream, milk, almond extract, and the remaining sugar together until the sugar is dissolved. Pour the mixture over the peaches.

Cover and cook on high for 1 hour and 45 minutes, or until the center is just set and jiggles slightly when the sides are tapped.

Uncover the cooker and remove the insert. Let cool slightly. Serve warm or at room temperature, scooping the flan out of the insert.

Creamy Cherry Clafoutis

Clafoutis is the French name for a batter cake made with fruit. It is quick to make and perfect for a homey family dessert.

This version uses cream cheese, so the texture is extra creamy and a little like a cheesecake. Try it with other soft fruits, such as apricots or berries.

SERVES 6

Unsalted butter

1 12-ounce bag frozen pitted cherries (about 2½ cups), thawed, or substitute fresh or drained canned cherries

6 ounces cream cheese, softened

2 large eggs

½ cup sugar

¼ cup all-purpose flour

¼ cup whole milk

½ teaspoon grated lemon zest

Confectioners' sugar

Generously butter the bottom and 2 inches up the sides of the insert of a large slow cooker. Scatter the cherries in the cooker.

In a food processor or blender, combine the cream cheese, eggs, sugar, flour, milk, and lemon zest. Process or blend until smooth and creamy. Pour the mixture over the cherries.

Cover and cook on high for 1½ to 2 hours, or until the center is just set. Sprinkle with confectioners' sugar and serve warm, scooping the clafoutis out of the insert.

Raspberry Brioche Pudding

After a long morning of shopping and museum-going in Paris, my husband and I stopped for lunch at a small café, where we enjoyed a sensational dessert of custardy *pain perdu,* or French toast, drizzled with raspberry sauce in a pool of cool custard. Here's my easy but equally wonderful version that you can make in the slow cooker. It's lovely with whipped cream or ice cream and fresh berries too.

SERVES 8

Unsalted butter

3 large eggs

¾ cup sugar

2 cups whole milk

1 cup heavy cream

1 teaspoon vanilla extract

6 ounces brioche or challah bread, cut into 1-inch cubes (about 6 cups)

¾ cup raspberry jam

Crème Anglaise (page 223), whipped cream, or ice cream (optional)

Generously butter the bottom and 2 inches up the sides of the insert of a large slow cooker.

In a large bowl, whisk together the eggs and sugar until pale and foamy. Beat in the milk, cream, and vanilla.

Scatter the bread cubes in the slow cooker. Pour the milk mixture over the bread. Avoiding the sides of the cooker, dot the surface with the jam.

Cover and cook on high for 3 hours, or until the center is just set. Serve warm with crème anglaise, if you like, scooping the pudding out of the insert.

Apricot French Bread Pudding

Dried apricots add a tangy sweet flavor and sunny color to this bread pudding. You can also substitute dried cherries, raisins, cranberries, or other fruits for the apricots.

Toasting the bread is not essential, but it gives the pudding a crunchy topping.

SERVES 8

- 8 ounces dried apricots
- Unsalted butter
- 6 large eggs
- ½ cup sugar
- 2½ cups whole milk
- 1½ teaspoons vanilla extract
- 1 teaspoon grated orange zest
- 6 ounces French bread, cut into 1-inch cubes and lightly toasted

Soak the apricots in warm water to cover for 20 minutes. Drain and pat dry. Cut the apricots into small pieces.

Butter the bottom and about 2 inches up the sides of the insert of a large slow cooker.

In a large bowl, whisk together the eggs and sugar until pale and foamy. Beat in the milk, vanilla, and orange zest. Stir in the apricots.

Scatter the bread cubes in the slow cooker. Pour the milk mixture over the bread and stir.

Cover and cook on high for 2½ to 3 hours, or until the center is just set. Serve warm, scooping the pudding from the dish.

Rice Pudding

In Paris one winter, *riz au lait* was a popular menu item at all the bistros. Why, I wondered, would anyone order something as mundane as rice pudding when everywhere I looked, there were flaky pastries, glistening fruit tarts, and sky-high soufflés from which to choose? Finally, my curiosity got the best of me, and I ordered it. And then I knew. It was far and away the best rice pudding I had ever tried, a creamy vanilla-scented perfection.

The secret is in the flavorings. A whole vanilla bean, instead of extract, gives the pudding a richer vanilla flavor, and orange zest adds a delicate perfume. I like this dessert best served slightly warm. Once it is chilled, it is still delicious, but the texture is much firmer.

SERVES 8

- 3 cups whole milk
- 1 cup heavy cream
- 1 whole vanilla bean
- ⅔ cup long-grain white rice (not converted rice)
- 1 2-inch strip orange zest
- Pinch of salt
- ½ cup sugar

Pour the milk and cream into the insert of a large slow cooker. With a small sharp knife, slit the vanilla bean lengthwise. Scrape out the seeds and add them to the cooker along with the vanilla pod. Stir in the rice, orange zest, and salt.

Cover and cook on high for 2½ to 3 hours, stirring two or three times to prevent the rice from sticking to the bottom, until the rice is tender. Stir in the sugar, cover, and cook for 20 minutes more.

Uncover and let cool to lukewarm before serving (it will thicken as it cools), or cover and refrigerate until chilled. Remove the orange zest and vanilla pod before serving.

Prune Custard Cake

In the Brittany region of northern France, this clafoutis made with plump, moist prunes is called *Far Breton*. Serve it with crème fraîche.

SERVES 6

¼ cup all-purpose flour

3 large eggs

½ cup sugar

1 cup whole milk

1 tablespoon Armagnac or cognac or 1 teaspoon rum extract

Pinch of salt

2 tablespoons unsalted butter, melted, plus more for the dish

⅔ cup pitted prunes

Put the flour, eggs, sugar, milk, Armagnac, salt, and melted butter in a food processor or blender. Process or blend until smooth, scraping down the sides of the container. Place the container in the refrigerator for at least 30 minutes.

Meanwhile, place the prunes in a bowl with hot water to cover. Let stand for 20 minutes. Drain and pat dry.

Butter a 6-cup soufflé dish that will fit inside a large slow cooker. Place a rack in the insert of the slow cooker (to improvise one, see page 9).

Scatter the prunes in the prepared dish. Carefully pour in the batter. Place the dish on the rack. Cover and cook on high for 2½ hours, or until the custard is set around the edges but slightly soft in the center. Let cool slightly. Carefully remove the dish from the slow cooker.

Cut into wedges and serve warm or at room temperature.

Orange Soufflé

Nothing is quite as elegant as a soufflé for dessert, and baking it in the slow cooker ensures that it will turn out just right. It does not rise as high as a baked soufflé, but it is very impressive nonetheless. Don't lift the cover while the souf- flé is baking, or it may collapse.

Serve with whipped cream or Crème Anglaise (page 223) and berries.

SERVES 4

Unsalted butter

5 large eggs, separated

Pinch of salt

¼ teaspoon cream of tartar

6 tablespoons sugar

2 tablespoons all-purpose flour

1 teaspoon grated orange zest

¼ cup fresh orange juice

2 tablespoons orange liqueur, such as Grand Marnier or Cointreau, or more orange juice

Generously butter a 6-cup soufflé dish.

In a large bowl with an electric mixer, beat the egg whites with the salt on me- dium speed until foamy. Add the cream of tartar and increase the speed to high. Gradually beat in 4 tablespoons of the sugar until stiff peaks form.

In a large bowl, whisk the egg yolks and the remaining 2 tablespoons sugar until light and pale-colored. Whisk in the flour and orange zest. Stir in the orange juice and liqueur.

With a rubber spatula, fold in one third of the egg whites. Gradually fold in the remaining whites. Scrape the mixture into the prepared dish.

Place a rack in the insert of a large slow cooker (to improvise one, see page 9). Place the soufflé dish on the rack. Pour hot water to a depth of 1 inch around the dish.

Cover and cook on high for 1½ hours, or until just set. Spoon the soufflé onto serving plates and serve.

Queen of Sheba Cake (Reine de Saba)

This cake is based on the famous Reine de Saba that helped launch my professional culinary career. While I was in college, I started to bake a version of this cake at home to supply a local gourmet shop and a restaurant in my Brooklyn neighborhood. Then one day I put a cake in the oven and set the timer. When I returned to the kitchen to remove it, the batter was still liquid and the oven had turned cold. Nothing could get it going again.

I hated to waste all of those good ingredients, so I improvised by placing a large pot partially filled with water on the stovetop. I put the cake pan on a rack in the pot, clamped on the lid, and steamed the cake until it was set.

I loved the tender, creamy texture of that steamed cake. My slow cooker does a great job of making a similar chocolate cake that is fit for a queen.

It looks great with just a sprinkling of confectioners' sugar, but when fresh raspberries are in season, I like to arrange them in rows on top of the cake as a garnish. Top with either whipped cream or Crème Anglaise (page 223).

SERVES 8

4   ounces semisweet or bittersweet chocolate

½   cup (1 stick) unsalted butter, softened, plus more for the dish

½   cup sugar

3   large eggs

1½   teaspoons vanilla extract

¾   cup finely ground toasted almonds

Butter a 7-inch springform pan. Line the bottom with a circle of parchment paper. Butter the paper. Place a rack in the insert of a large slow cooker (to improvise one, see page 9).

Melt the chocolate in the top of a double boiler or in a heatproof bowl set over a pan of simmering water. The bottom of the bowl should not touch the water. Let stand for a few minutes until softened. Stir until completely melted.

In a large bowl with an electric mixer, beat the butter with the sugar on medium speed until light and fluffy. Beat in the eggs one at a time and add the vanilla. With a rubber spatula, gently fold in the chocolate and almonds.

Scrape the mixture into the prepared pan. Place the pan on the rack. Pour just enough hot water into the cooker so that it stays below the bottom of the pan.

Cover and cook on high for 2 hours, or until the cake is slightly soft in the center and set around the edges. Remove the pan from the cooker and let cool slightly.

Cover and chill for several hours or overnight. Run a small knife around the edge of the cake. Remove the sides of the pan. Cut into wedges and serve.

Corsican Honey Cheesecake

I've been to Corsica only once, for a very short time, but I remember having a delightful lunch followed by a honey-flavored cheesecake. In Corsica, cheesecake is made with a fresh ricotta-like sheep's- or goat's-milk cheese called *brocciu*, pronounced "broach." A blend of ricotta and cream cheese has a similar flavor and texture. Use an aromatic honey for the best flavor.

SERVES 6

    Unsalted butter
1 **15-ounce container whole-milk ricotta cheese**
6 **ounces cream cheese, softened**
⅓ **cup honey**
2 **large eggs**
1 **teaspoon grated lemon zest**
1 **teaspoon vanilla extract**

Butter a 7-inch springform pan. Place the pan on a large sheet of aluminum foil and wrap the foil around the sides so that water cannot enter.

In a food processor or blender, process or blend the ricotta and cream cheese with the honey until very smooth. Add the eggs, lemon zest, and vanilla and process until blended. Pour the mixture into the prepared pan.

Place a rack in the insert of a large slow cooker (to improvise one, see page 9). Place the pan on the rack. Pour hot water to a depth of 1 inch around the pan. Cover and cook on high for 2½ hours, or until the cheesecake is set around the edges but soft and jiggly in the center. Remove the pan and let the cake cool slightly on a rack. Cover and refrigerate for at least 2 hours or overnight.

Run a knife around the edge of the cheesecake. Remove the sides of the pan. Cut into wedges and serve.

Chocolate Pain Perdu (Chocolate Bread Pudding)

The combination of bread and chocolate—whether in the form of the classic French child's after-school snack of a chocolate bar stuffed into a baguette, or fresh bread served with a cup of thick, steaming hot chocolate, or a chocolate-filled croissant—is a match made in heaven. This bread pudding is no exception. Serve it warm with ice cream.

SERVES 8

	Unsalted butter
1	**baguette, cut into 1-inch cubes (about 6 cups)**
2	**cups whole milk**
10	**ounces semisweet or bittersweet chocolate, chopped**
4	**large eggs**
½	**cup sugar**
1	**cup heavy cream**
1	**teaspoon vanilla extract**
	Ice cream, whipped cream, or Crème Anglaise (page 223)

Butter the bottom and 2 inches up the sides of the insert of a large slow cooker. Scatter the bread cubes in the cooker.

Heat the milk in a small pan over medium heat until small bubbles form around the edges. Remove it from the heat. Set aside ¼ cup of the chopped chocolate. Add the remaining chocolate to the hot milk and stir until smooth and melted.

In a large bowl, beat the eggs and sugar until foamy. Beat in the chocolate milk, cream, and vanilla.

Pour the milk mixture over the bread in the cooker. Scatter the reserved ¼ cup chocolate pieces on top. Cover and cook on high for 3 hours, or until softly set in the center.

Let cool slightly. Scoop the pudding from the dish and serve with ice cream.

Basics

Croutons 216

Aioli 217

Rouille 218

Pesto 219

Vinaigrette/Citronette 220

Tomato Sauce 221

Pipérade 222

Crème Anglaise 223

Croutons

In soup or salad, homemade croutons are so much better than the packaged kind. These are hard to resist, and I often find myself snacking on them too.

MAKES ABOUT 3 CUPS

- 4 slices brioche, challah, or good-quality white bread, cut into ¾-inch cubes
- 3 tablespoons unsalted butter, melted, or olive oil
  Salt and freshly ground pepper

Preheat the oven to 350°F. Spread the bread cubes on a large baking sheet. Drizzle with the butter and sprinkle with salt and pepper to taste. Bake, stirring occasionally, until lightly toasted, about 10 minutes. Remove and let cool completely. (The croutons can be made up to 2 days ahead and stored in a plastic bag at room temperature.)

Variations

HERB CROUTONS: Add 1 teaspoon herbes de Provence, dried thyme, or crumbled dried rosemary to the butter before drizzling.

PARMESAN CROUTONS: Sprinkle with ½ cup freshly grated Parmigiano-Reggiano before baking.

FRENCH OR SOURDOUGH CROUTONS: Tear crusty French or sourdough bread into bite-size chunks and proceed as directed. The torn edges give the croutons extra crunch.

Aioli

Golden yellow, smooth as satin, and redolent of garlic, this luxurious sauce is a mayonnaise flavored with garlic. Aioli is heavenly with Chicken in the Pot (page 53), grilled salmon, or steamed vegetables.

For a Provençal-style summer fete, serve your family or guests a Grand Aioli, also called *aioli monstre*: piles of raw and cooked vegetables, such as carrots, green beans, potatoes, baby beets, and turnips; sliced meats or chicken; or poached fish and seafood—with a big bowl of this sauce, French bread, and chilled rosé or white wine.

The eggs in this recipe are not cooked, so if you are concerned about this, substitute pasteurized eggs, which are widely available.

MAKES 1½ CUPS

- 2 large garlic cloves, or to taste, peeled
- ½ teaspoon salt
- 2 large egg yolks
- 1 teaspoon Dijon mustard
- 1 cup extra-virgin olive oil (for a milder flavor, use a blend of olive oil and vegetable oil)
- 1–2 teaspoons fresh lemon juice

In a food processor, combine the garlic and salt and process until finely chopped. With the machine running, add the egg yolks and mustard and process until smooth. Very slowly drizzle in the oil. It's important to go slowly so that the sauce comes out smooth and does not break. Once you have added ½ cup of the oil, you can add the remainder a little more rapidly. Add the lemon juice to taste.

If the sauce should curdle, place a tablespoon of mustard in a bowl, then with a whisk gradually beat in the sauce a spoonful at a time. Serve immediately or store in a covered jar in the refrigerator for up to 2 days.

Rouille

You can make this luscious rosy red pepper sauce from scratch by first whipping up your own mayonnaise and then adding roasted peppers, but I like this convenient shortcut method just as well. Serve it with Bouillabaisse (page 122) or grilled swordfish, as a dip for raw vegetables or shrimp, or as a spread for sandwiches.

MAKES 1¾ CUPS

- ½ cup roasted red bell peppers, jarred or homemade
- 1 large garlic clove, peeled
- 1 cup mayonnaise
- 2 tablespoons extra-virgin olive oil
- 1 teaspoon fresh lemon juice
- Pinch of piment d'Espelette (see page 18) or cayenne

In a blender or food processor, finely chop the peppers and garlic together. Add the mayonnaise, oil, lemon juice, and piment d'Espelette and process until smooth. Serve immediately or store in a covered jar in the refrigerator for up to 2 days.

Pesto

No matter how you use it, you can't go wrong with a container of pesto in the refrigerator or freezer. If the oil separates, just stir it before using. Add the sauce to hot or cold soup; toss it with cooked potatoes, green beans, or zucchini; spoon it over soft goat cheese, sliced tomatoes, or grilled chicken; stir it into mayonnaise or cream cheese; toss it with pasta; or spread it on a sandwich.

Unlike Italian-style pesto, this Provençal version does not contain nuts or cheese, though you can add some Parmigiano-Reggiano or Emmental, if you like. The parsley helps the sauce keep its brilliant green color.

I've heard French cooks say that basil for *pistou* should *not* be fresh-picked. Yesterday's basil, they contend, has lost some of its moisture, so the flavor is more concentrated. True or not, the assertion makes me feel better about turning to store-bought basil when I have none fresh from my garden.

MAKES 1 CUP

1½ cups fresh basil leaves, washed and well dried

1 cup fresh flat-leaf parsley, washed and well dried

3 garlic cloves, peeled

Coarse sea salt or kosher salt

⅓ cup extra-virgin olive oil

In a food processor or blender, combine the herbs and garlic and process until finely chopped. Add salt to taste. Blend in the oil. Taste for seasoning.

Serve immediately or cover and refrigerate for up to 3 days.

Vinaigrette/Citronette

Vinaigrette or citronette, as the lemon version is called, is the ultimate French salad dressing, though it is pressed into service in countless other ways, such as drizzled over poached or grilled fish or used as a marinade. Once you've tasted this dressing made with fresh ingredients, nothing else will do. Fortunately, it takes just minutes to prepare.

The basic proportions are 1 part vinegar or lemon juice to 3 parts oil, but you can adjust according to your taste.

MAKES ABOUT 1 CUP

6 tablespoons extra-virgin olive oil

2 tablespoons red wine vinegar, sherry vinegar, or fresh lemon juice

1 teaspoon Dijon mustard

Salt and freshly ground pepper

Combine all the ingredients in a jar with a tight-fitting lid. Cover and shake until well blended. Taste for seasoning.

Variations

Use all or part walnut, grapeseed, or vegetable oil.

Use balsamic, champagne, raspberry, or other flavored vinegar.

Add 1 tablespoon of finely chopped shallot, scallion, or fresh herbs.

Tomato Sauce

Fresh tomatoes or good canned tomatoes (see page 19) make an excellent quick sauce to serve with eggs, fish, meat, or chicken.

MAKES ABOUT 2 CUPS

- 2 tablespoons unsalted butter or olive oil
- 2 tablespoons minced shallots
- 3 pounds fresh plum tomatoes, peeled (see page 18), seeded, and chopped, or one 28-ounce can Italian whole tomatoes with their juice, passed through a food mill
- ½ teaspoon chopped fresh thyme
- Salt and freshly ground pepper

In a medium saucepan, melt the butter over medium heat. Add the shallots and cook for 1 to 2 minutes, until they are translucent. Add the tomatoes and thyme and season with salt and pepper to taste. Bring to a simmer, lower the heat, and cook until the sauce is slightly thickened, about 10 minutes. Serve hot.

Pipérade

In France's Basque region, this delicious sauce is served with just about everything from omelets to sautéed chicken. Try scrambling some eggs and cooking them in the sauce or poaching some fish in it. It is also good tossed with pasta.

MAKES 3½ CUPS

- 2 tablespoons olive oil
- 4 ounces chopped ham
- 2 medium onions, halved and thinly sliced
- 3 garlic cloves, finely chopped
- 2 red or green bell peppers, thinly sliced
- 1½ teaspoons chopped fresh thyme
- Salt
- 2 cups chopped peeled (see page 18) and seeded fresh tomatoes or chopped canned tomatoes
- 2 teaspoons piment d'Espelette (see page 18) or paprika

In a large skillet, heat the oil over medium-high heat. Add the ham and cook, stirring occasionally, until lightly browned. With a slotted spoon, remove the ham to a plate.

Reduce the heat to medium. Add the onions to the skillet and cook, stirring often, until tender and golden, about 8 minutes. Stir in the garlic, then add the bell peppers, thyme, and salt to taste. Cover and cook, stirring once or twice, until the peppers are softened, about 10 minutes.

Add the ham, tomatoes, and piment d'Espelette and stir well. Bring to a simmer and cook for 10 minutes, or until the sauce is slightly thickened. Serve hot.

Crème Anglaise

The ultimate dessert sauce, custard cream is good enough to eat with a spoon. In fact, I often do! If you want to, you can pour it into an ice-cream maker for perfect vanilla ice cream. As a sauce, it is amazingly scrumptious with berries, fruit tarts, cakes, and anything chocolate.

MAKES 2½ CUPS

1 cup heavy cream

1 cup whole milk

1 vanilla bean or 1½ teaspoons vanilla extract

3 large egg yolks

⅓ cup sugar

Pinch of salt

Combine the cream and milk in a small saucepan. Split the vanilla bean lengthwise with a small sharp knife. Scrape the seeds out of the vanilla bean and into the cream mixture. Add the vanilla pod. (If using the vanilla extract, add it as the sauce is cooling.)

Cook the cream mixture over medium heat until small bubbles appear around the edge. Remove from the heat and let stand for 5 minutes. Remove the vanilla pod and discard.

In a heatproof bowl, whisk the egg yolks, sugar, and salt. Gradually whisk in the warm cream mixture. Transfer the sauce to the saucepan. Cook over low heat, stirring constantly, until small wisps of steam appear on the surface and the sauce coats the back of a spoon. (Test it by dipping a spoon in the sauce and carefully—it's hot—running your finger down the back of the spoon. If it leaves a distinct track, the sauce is done.) Do not allow the sauce to boil, or it may curdle.

Immediately pour the sauce into a clean bowl set into a larger bowl of ice water. Let cool, stirring occasionally. Cover and refrigerate until serving time or for up to 2 days.

Index

aioli, 217
    chicken in the pot with, 53
almonds:
    Moroccan chicken with apricots and, 59
    Queen of Sheba cake (Reine de Saba),
        210–12, *211*
Alsatian dishes:
    choucroute garni (sausages with sauerkraut),
        114–15, *115*
    lentil soup with bratwurst, 38
anchovy (fillets):
    creamy white bean *brandade*, *178*, 179
    dressing, 62
    potatoes pissaladière, 164
appetizers:
    chicken liver mousse, silky, 64–66, *65*
    country pâté, 107–8
    rillettes (spiced potted pork), 104–6, *105*
    white bean *brandade*, creamy, *178*, 179
apples:
    braised red cabbage with chestnuts and,
        156, 157
    Normandy pork with, 113
apricot(s):
    French bread pudding, 206
    Moroccan chicken with almonds and, 59
artichoke(s):
    hearts, in vegetable bouquet, 157
    lamb with olives and, 100

bacon:
    and Gruyère *pain perdu*, *146*, 147–48
    Parisian split pea soup with croutons and, 33
    warm lentil salad with vinaigrette and, 174
Baking (Greenspan), 202
bargemen's beef stew, 81

basil, in pesto, 219
Basque dishes:
    chicken with ham and sweet peppers, 56
    meatballs Bayonnaise with spicy tomato and
        pepper sauce, 92–93, *93*
    pipérade, 222
    tuna and potato stew, 129
Bayonnaise meatballs with spicy tomato and
    pepper sauce, 92–93, *93*
bean(s):
    Bretonne, 176
    and cabbage soup (*garbure*), 39
    chickpeas, in Moroccan vegetable couscous,
        180–81, *181*
    dried, 14–16
    à la française, 175
    pork, lamb and (cassoulet), 110–12, *111*
    salad, warm, with mustard vinaigrette, 177
    soupe au pistou, 28, *29*
    white, *brandade*, creamy, *178*, 179
Beard, James, 162
beef, 7, 79–93
    brisket, spiced, with carrots and turnips,
        82–83, *83*
    broth, classic French, 41
    meatballs, Roussillon, 91
    meatballs Bayonnaise with spicy tomato and
        pepper sauce, 92–93, *93*
    pot roast, red wine–braised, 79–80
    short ribs with dark beer and shallots, 90
    short ribs with red wine and prunes,
        88–89, *89*
    stew, bargemen's, 81
    stew, Provençal, with black olives, 84–85
    stew with mushrooms, rosemary, and toma-
        toes, 86–87, *87*

beer, dark:
   short ribs with shallots and, 90
   spiced beef brisket with carrots and turnips,
      82–83, *83*
beet(s), "roasted":
   with butter and herbs, 153
   salad with Roquefort and walnuts, 154, *155*
bisque, butternut, *24*, 25
blue cheeses, 13
   Roquefort, "roasted" beet salad with walnuts
      and, 154, *155*
boeuf en daube, 86
bouillabaisse, 122–23, *123*
   chicken, 57
   spinach and egg, 34–35
bourride (creamy fish soup), 36–37, *37*
brandade, creamy white bean, *178*, 179
bratwurst, Alsatian lentil soup with, 38
bread crumbs, as thickener, 4, 9
bread pudding. *See pain perdu*
Bretonne dishes:
   beans, 176
   prune custard cake, 208
brioche pudding, raspberry, 204, *205*
broccoli, in crustless vegetable quiche, 142, *143*
broths:
   beef, classic French, 41
   chicken, 40
   fennel and tomato, mussels in, *vi*, 121
   salt content of, 8
browning meats and vegetables, 4, 8
butter:
   escargot, chicken with, 52
   maître d'hôtel, halibut with, 128
   truffle, 19
   truffle, in chicken in half mourning, *50*, 51
butternut squash:
   bisque, *24*, 25
   gratin, 165

cabbage:
   and bean soup (*garbure*), 39
   choucroute garni (sausages with sauerkraut),
      114–15, *115*
   red, braised, with apples and chestnuts, *156*, 157
cakes:
   cherry clafoutis, creamy, 203
   honey cheesecake, Corsican, 213
   prune custard, 208

Queen of Sheba (Reine de Saba), 210–12, *211*
calamari Niçoise with black olives, *130*, 131
carrot(s), 8
   "roasted" root vegetables, 168
   soup, hot or cold, with tarragon whipped
      cream, 31
   spiced beef brisket with turnips and,
      82–83, *83*
cassoulet (pork, lamb, and beans), 110–12, *111*
Catalan cauliflower and potatoes, 158
cauliflower:
   Moroccan vegetable couscous, 180–81, *181*
   and potatoes Catalan, 158
   saffron vegetable stew, 169
   soup with caviar, 32
caviar, cauliflower soup with, 32
celery, 8
cheese, 13–14. *See also* goat cheese
   crustless vegetable quiche, 142, *143*
   Gruyère and bacon *pain perdu*, *146*, 147–48
   ham and, crustless quiche, 135
   mushroom *pain perdu*, 149
   Parmesan croutons, 216
   polenta with ham, tomato sauce and, 182, *183*
   potato and herb gratin, 162
   Roquefort, "roasted" beet salad with walnuts
      and, 154, *155*
   sheep's-milk, polenta with crème fraîche and,
      184
   soufflé, fallen, 136–37
   spinach soufflé, 140–41
cheesecake, honey, Corsican, 213
cherry clafoutis, creamy, 203
chestnuts, braised red cabbage with apples and,
      156, 157
chèvre. *See* goat cheese
chicken, 7, 8, 42–63
   Basque, with ham and sweet peppers, 56
   bouillabaisse, 57
   broth, 40
   Corsican, with sun-dried tomatoes, 55
   with escargot butter, 52
   with figs, 60–61
   with forty cloves of garlic, 58
   in half mourning, *50*, 51
   herbed roast, with garlic and shallots, 47
   Moroccan, with apricots and almonds, 59
   pan bagnat (Niçoise chicken sandwich),
      62–63, *63*

in the pot with aioli, 53
salad Parisienne, 48, *49*
Sunday roast, with potatoes, lemon, and
thyme, 45–46, *46*
with tarragon, mustard, and cream, 54
chicken liver(s):
country pâté, 107–8
mousse, silky, 64–66, *65*
chickpeas, in Moroccan vegetable couscous,
180–81, *181*
chocolate:
bittersweet, creams, *196*, 197
pain perdu (chocolate bread pudding), 214
Queen of Sheba cake (Reine de Saba),
210–12, *211*
choucroute garni (sausages with sauerkraut),
114–15, *115*
citronette, 220
clafoutis:
cherry, creamy, 203
prune custard cake, 208
clams, in bouillabaisse, 122–23, *123*
confit. *See* duck confit
cornichons, 14
Cornish hens, Dijon-style, with mustard sauce,
68, 69
cornmeal. *See* polenta
Corsican dishes:
chicken with sun-dried tomatoes, 55
honey cheesecake, 213
country pâté, 107–8
couscous, Moroccan vegetable, 180–81, *181*
creams:
bittersweet chocolate, *196*, 197
lemon pots de crème, *194*, *195*
crème anglaise, 223
crème brûlée:
ginger, 200–201
vanilla, 201
crème caramel, bistro, 198–99, *199*
crème fraîche, 14
croutons, 216
curried pork, spicy, 103

desserts, 3, 188–214. *See also* cakes
apricot French bread pudding, 206
bittersweet chocolate creams, *196*, 197
chocolate *pain perdu* (chocolate bread pudding), 214

crème anglaise, 223
crème caramel, bistro, 198–99, *199*
ginger crème brûlée, 200–201
lemon pots de crème, 194, *195*
orange soufflé, 209
peach flan, 202
pears, honeyed, with goat cheese and thyme,
192, 193
pears, tea-spiced, 191
raspberry brioche pudding, 204, *205*
rice pudding, 207
vanilla crème brûlée, 201
Dijon-style Cornish hens with mustard sauce,
68, 69
dressings:
anchovy, 62
mustard vinaigrette, 177
vinaigrette, 160
vinaigrette/citronette, 220
duck, 44
confit, 72–73
confit, crispy, 74, *75*
confit, in cassoulet (pork, lamb, and beans),
110–12, *111*
fat, 16, 72
duxelles-stuffed turkey breast, 70–71

egg(s), 132–49. *See also pain perdu*; quiches,
crustless; soufflés
and spinach bouillabaisse, 34–35
tomato and goat cheese flan, 144, *145*
Emmental, 13. *See also* cheese
escargot butter, chicken with, 52
Espelette pepper (piment d'Espelette), 18, 56

fallen cheese soufflé, 136–37
far Breton, 208
fat, skimming, 9
fennel:
and tomato broth, mussels in, *vi*, 121
tomato soup, 26
figs, chicken with, 60–61
first courses. *See* appetizers; soups
fish, 2, 8, 122–29. *See also* salmon; seafood
fillets, in bouillabaisse, 122–23, *123*
halibut with maître d'hôtel butter, 128
soup, creamy (*bourride*), 36–37, *37*
tuna and potato stew, Basque, 129
flageolet beans, 16

flans:
  peach, 202
  tomato and goat cheese, 144, *145*
frozen foods, safety concerns and, 11

garbure (cabbage and bean soup), 39
garlic:
  aioli, 217
  buying, 23
  chicken with forty cloves of, 58
  "roasted" root vegetables, 168
  soup, 23
ginger crème brûlée, 200–201
goat cheese (chèvre), 13
  honeyed pears with thyme and, *192*, 193
  summer *tian* with thyme and, 166
  and tomato flan, 144, *145*
  and walnut soufflé, 138–39
grains, 172, 180–87. *See also* pilafs; polenta
  couscous, Moroccan vegetable, 180–81, *181*
grand aioli (*aioli monstre*), 217
gratins, 2–3
  butternut squash, 165
  potato and herb, 162
  potatoes pissaladière, 164
green beans, in chicken salad Parisienne, 48, *49*
Greenspan, Dorie, 202
Gruyère, 13. *See also* cheese

halibut with maître d'hôtel butter, 128
ham:
  Basque chicken with sweet peppers and, 56
  and cheese quiche, crustless, 135
  pipérade, 222
  polenta with cheese, tomato sauce and, 182, *183*
Haute-Savoie polenta with sheep's-milk cheese
    and crème fraîche, 184
Henri IV, King, 53
herb(ed)(s), 4, 8, 16–17
  croutons, 216
herbes de Provence, 17
honey(ed):
  cheesecake, Corsican, 213
  pears with goat cheese and thyme, *192*, 193
hunter's-style pork ribs, 116–17, *117*

ingredients:
  French pantry, 13–19
  tips for, 8–9

juniper berries, 17

lamb, 7, 98–102
  with artichokes and olives, 100
  pork, and beans (cassoulet), 110–12, *111*
  shanks with lentils and mustard, 101
  stew with spring vegetables (*navarin printa-
    nier*), 98–99
  you can eat with a spoon, 102
leek(s), 17
  potato soup, two-way, 30
legumes, 170–79. *See also* bean(s); lentil(s)
lemon pots de crème, 194, *195*
lentil(s):
  basic, 173
  lamb shanks with mustard and, 101
  salad, warm, with bacon and vinaigrette, 174
  with scallions, 173
  soup with bratwurst, Alsatian, 38

Made in Marseille (Young), 64
maître d'hôtel butter, halibut with, 128
Marengo, veal, 97
marmitako, 129
meatballs:
  Bayonnaise with spicy tomato and pepper
    sauce, 92–93, *93*
  Roussillon, 91
  spinach, Provençal, 67
meats, 7, 8, 76–117. *See also* beef; lamb; pork;
  veal
Menus for Entertaining (Beard), 162
mint, salmon with tomatoes and, 127
monkfish, in *bourride* (creamy fish soup),
    36–37, *37*
Moroccan dishes:
  chicken with apricots and almonds, 59
  vegetable couscous, 180–81, *181*
mousse, silky chicken liver, 64–66, *65*
mushroom(s):
  beef stew with rosemary, tomatoes and,
    86–87, *87*
  duxelles-stuffed turkey breast, 70–71
  pain perdu, 149
  pork ribs hunter's style, 116–17, *117*
  pork with cream and, 109
  spelt pilaf with, 187
mussels in fennel and tomato broth, *vi*, 121
mustard, 17

chicken with tarragon, cream and, 54
lamb shanks with lentils and, 101
salmon steaks with parsley and, 126
sauce, Dijon-style Cornish hens with, *68*, 69
vinaigrette, 177

navarin printanier (lamb stew with spring
    vegetables), 98–99
Niçoise dishes:
    calamari with black olives, *130*, 131
    chicken *pan bagnat* (chicken sandwich),
        62–63, *63*
    warm bean salad with mustard vinaigrette,
        177
Normandy pork with apples, 113

olive oil, extra-virgin, 16
olives, 17
    black, calamari Niçoise with, *130*, 131
    black, in potatoes pissaladière, 164
    black, lamb with artichokes and, 100
    black, Provençal beef stew with, 84–85
    green, in Roussillon meatballs, 91
    green, slow-cooked salmon with lemon
        and, 124–25, *125*
onion(s), 8, 17–18
    pearl, in *navarin printanier* (lamb stew with
        spring vegetables), 98–99
    potatoes pissaladière, 164
    saffron vegetable stew, 169
    sauce, veal shanks with, 96
orange soufflé, 209
osso buco, French version of, 96

pain perdu (bread pudding):
    apricot French bread, 206
    bacon and Gruyère, *146*, 147–48
    chocolate, 214
    mushroom, 149
    raspberry brioche, 204, *205*
pan bagnat, chicken (Niçoise chicken sand-
    wich), 62–63, *63*
Parisian dishes:
    chicken salad, 48, *49*
    split pea soup with bacon and croutons, 33
Parmesan croutons, 216
Parmigiano-Reggiano, 14
parsley, 8
pâtés, 3, 7

chicken liver mousse, silky, 64–66, *65*
    country, 107–8
    rillettes (spiced potted pork), 104–6, *105*
pea, split, soup with bacon and croutons, Pari-
    sian, 33
peach flan, 202
pears:
    honeyed, with goat cheese and thyme, *192*,
        193
    tea-spiced, 191
pepper(s). *See also* Espelette pepper
    Basque chicken with ham and, 56
    pipérade, 222
    rouille, 218
    and tomato sauce, spicy, meatballs Bayonnaise
        with, 92–93, *93*
pesto, 219
    Provençal vegetable soup with (*soupe au
        pistou*), 28, *29*
pilafs:
    rice, 185
    rice, with golden raisins and pistachios, 186
    spelt, with mushrooms, 187
piment d'Espelette (Espelette pepper), 18, 56
pipérade, 222
    potatoes, 163
pissaladière, potatoes, 164
pistachios, rice pilaf with golden raisins and,
    186
polenta:
    with ham, cheese, and tomato sauce, 182, *183*
    with sheep's-milk cheese and crème fraîche,
        184
pork, 7, 103–17. *See also* bacon; ham; sausages
    country pâté, 107–8
    lamb, and beans (cassoulet), 110–12, *111*
    with mushrooms and cream, 109
    Normandy, with apples, 113
    ribs hunter's style, 116–17, *117*
    Roussillon meatballs, 91
    spiced potted (rillettes), 104–6, *105*
    spicy curried, 103
potato(es), 8
    and cauliflower, Catalan, 158
    chicken salad Parisienne, 48, *49*
    and herb gratin, 162
    leek soup, two-way, 30
    new, with butter and herbs, 159
    pipérade, 163

potato(es) *cont.*
pissaladière, 164
"roasted" root vegetables, 168
saffron vegetable stew, 169
salad, French, 160, *161*
spinach and egg bouillabaisse, 34–35
summer *tian* with goat cheese and thyme, 166
and tuna stew, Basque, 129
vegetable bouquet, 157, 167
pot roast, red wine–braised, 79–80
pots de crème, lemon, 194, *195*
power outages, 11
Provençal dishes:
beef stew with black olives, 84–85
chicken bouillabaisse, 57
potatoes pissaladière, 164
saffron vegetable stew, 169
salmon with tomatoes and mint, 127
spinach and egg bouillabaisse, 34–35
spinach meatballs, 67
vegetable soup with pesto (*soupe au pistou*), 28, *29*
prune(s):
custard cake, 208
short ribs with red wine and, 88–89, *89*
puddings. *See also pain perdu*
rice, 207

Queen of Sheba cake (Reine de Saba), 210–12, *211*
quiches, crustless, 2
ham and cheese, 135
vegetable, 142, *143*

raisins, golden, rice pilaf with pistachios and, 186
raspberry brioche pudding, 204, *205*
red cabbage, braised, with apples and chestnuts, *156*, 157
red wine, 19
–braised pot roast, 79–80
short ribs with prunes and, 88–89, *89*
reheating foods, 11
Reine de Saba (Queen of Sheba cake), 210–12, *211*
ribs:
pork, hunter's style, 116–17, *117*
short, with dark beer and shallots, 90
short, with red wine and prunes, 88–89, *89*

rice:
pilaf, 185
pilaf with golden raisins and pistachios, 186
pudding, 207
rillettes (spiced potted pork), 104–6, *105*
root vegetables, 8. *See also specific* roots
"roasted," 168
Roquefort, "roasted" beet salad with walnuts and, 154, *155*
rouille, 218
Roussillon meatballs, 91

safety concerns, 11
temperature of cooked food, 7, 11
saffron vegetable stew, 169
salads:
bean, warm, with mustard vinaigrette, 177
beet, "roasted," with Roquefort and walnuts, 154, *155*
chicken, Parisienne, 48, *49*
lentil, warm, with bacon and vinaigrette, 174
potato, French, 160, *161*
salmon:
slow-cooked, with lemon and green olives, 124–25, *125*
steaks with mustard and parsley, 126
with tomatoes and mint, 127
salt, 8
sandwich, Niçoise chicken (chicken *pan bagnat*), 62–63, *63*
sauces:
aioli, 217
crème anglaise, 223
pesto, 219
pipérade, 222
rouille, 218
tomato, 221
sauerkraut, sausages with (*choucroute garni*), 114–15, *115*
sausages:
bratwurst, Alsatian lentil soup with, 38
cassoulet (pork, lamb, and beans), 110–12, *111*
with sauerkraut (*choucroute garni*), 114–15, *115*
scallops, sea:
bouillabaisse, 122–23, *123*
bourride (creamy fish soup), 36–37, *37*
seafood, 2, 8, 118–31. *See also* fish; salmon
bouillabaisse, 122–23, *123*
bourride (creamy fish soup), 36–37, *37*

calamari Niçoise with black olives, *130*, 131
mussels in fennel and tomato broth, *vi*, 121
shallots, 17–18
    "roasted" root vegetables, 168
    short ribs with dark beer and, 90
sheep's-milk cheese, polenta with crème fraîche
    and, 184
short ribs:
    with dark beer and shallots, 90
    with red wine and prunes, 88–89, *89*
shrimp, in bouillabaisse, 122–23, *123*
sides. *See also* pilafs; vegetable(s)
    bean salad, warm, with mustard vinaigrette,
      177
    beans à la française, 175
    beans Bretonne, 176
    lentils, basic, 173
    lentil salad, warm, with bacon and vinai-
      grette, 174
    lentils with scallions, 173
    white bean *brandade*, creamy, *178*, 179
slow cookers:
    adapting recipes for, 4
    choosing, 5–6
    cooking times for, 7
    reasons to use, 3
    safety concerns and, 11
    tips and techniques for, 7–9
soufflés, 2
    cheese, fallen, 136–37
    goat cheese and walnut, 138–39
    orange, 209
    spinach, 140–41
soups, 2, 4, 8–9, 20–41. *See also* broths
    butternut bisque, *24*, 25
    cabbage and bean (*garbure*), 39
    carrot, hot or cold, with tarragon whipped
      cream, 31
    cauliflower, with caviar, 32
    chicken bouillabaisse, 57
    fish, creamy (*bourride*), 36–37, *37*
    garlic, 23
    lentil, Alsatian, with bratwurst, 38
    potato-leek, two-way, 30
    spinach and egg bouillabaisse, 34–35
    split pea, with bacon and croutons, Parisian, 33
    tomato-fennel, 26
    vegetable, Provençal, with pesto (*soupe au
      pistou*), 28, *29*

zucchini, creamy, 27
southwestern France, dishes from:
    crispy duck confit, 74
    garbure (cabbage and bean soup), 39
spelt, 18
    pilaf with mushrooms, 187
spices, 8
spinach:
    and egg bouillabaisse, 34–35
    meatballs, Provençal, 67
    soufflé, 140–41
split pea soup with bacon and croutons, Pari-
    sian, 33
spreads:
    chicken liver mousse, silky, 64–66, *65*
    rillettes (spiced potted pork), 104–6, *105*
    white bean *brandade*, creamy, *178*, 179
spring vegetables:
    lamb stew with (*navarin printanier*), 98–99
    vegetable bouquet, 167
stews, 1, 2, 4, 8–9
    beef, bargemen's, 81
    beef, Provençal, with black olives, 84–85
    beef, with mushrooms, rosemary, and toma-
      toes, 86–87, *87*
    bouillabaisse, 122–23, *123*
    cassoulet (pork, lamb, and beans), 110–12, *111*
    lamb, with spring vegetables (*navarin printa-
      nier*), 98–99
    pork, spicy curried, 103
    pork with mushrooms and cream, 109
    tuna and potato, Basque, 129
    veal, white (veal blanquette), 94–95
    vegetable, saffron, 169
summer *tian* with goat cheese and thyme, 166
Sunday roast chicken with potatoes, lemon, and
    thyme, 45–46, *46*

tarragon whipped cream, 31
tea-spiced pears, 191
temperature of cooked food, 7, 11
thickening soups and stews, 4, 8 9
tian, summer, with goat cheese and thyme, 166
timing tips, 7
tomato(es), 18–19
    beef stew with mushrooms, rosemary and,
      86 87, *87*
    and fennel broth, mussels in, *vi*, 121
    fennel soup, 26

tomato(es) *cont.*
and goat cheese flan, 144, *145*
peeling, 18
and pepper sauce, spicy, meatballs Bayonnaise
with, 92–93, *93*
pipérade, 222
potatoes pissaladière, 164
saffron vegetable stew, 169
salmon with mint and, 127
sauce, 221
sauce, polenta with ham, cheese and, 182, *183*
summer *tian* with goat cheese and thyme, 166
sun-dried, Corsican chicken with, 55
veal Marengo, 97
truffle(s), 19
butter, in chicken in half mourning, *50*, 51
tuna and potato stew, Basque, 129
turkey, 7, 44
breast, duxelles-stuffed, 70–71
country pâté, 107–8
Provençal spinach meatballs, 67
turnips, 8
navarin printanier (lamb stew with spring
vegetables), 98–99
"roasted" root vegetables, 168
spiced beef brisket with carrots and,
82–83, *83*

vanilla crème brûlée, 201
veal, 94–97
blanquette (white veal stew), 94–95
Marengo, 97
shanks with onion sauce, 96
vegetable(s), 2–3, 8, 150–69
beet, "roasted," salad with Roquefort and walnuts, 154, *155*
beets, "roasted," with butter and herbs, 153
bouquet, 167
butternut squash gratin, 165
cauliflower and potatoes Catalan, 158
couscous, Moroccan, 180–81, *181*
potato and herb gratin, 162
potatoes, new, with butter and herbs, 159
potatoes pipérade, 163
potatoes pissaladière, 164

potato salad, French, 160, *161*
quiche, crustless, 142, *143*
red cabbage, braised, with apples and chestnuts, *156*, 157
root, "roasted," 168
soup with pesto, Provençal (*soupe au pistou*),
28, *29*
spring, lamb stew with (*navarin printanier*),
98–99
stew, saffron, 169
summer *tian* with goat cheese and thyme, 166
vegetarian main dishes:
crustless vegetable quiche, 142
fallen cheese soufflé, 136–37
goat cheese and walnut soufflé, 138–39
Moroccan vegetable couscous, 180–81
mushroom pain perdu, 149
polenta with sheep's-milk cheese and crème
fraîche, 184
roasted beet salad with Roquefort and walnuts, 154
saffron vegetable stew, 169
spinach soufflé, 140–41
summer tian with goat cheese and thyme, 166
tomato and goat cheese flan, 144
vinaigrette, 160, 220
mustard, 177

walnut(s):
and goat cheese soufflé, 138–39
"roasted" beet salad with Roquefort and,
154, *155*
whipped cream, tarragon, 31
white beans. *See* bean(s)
wine, 19
red, –braised pot roast, 79–80
red, short ribs with prunes and, 88–89, *89*

Young, Daniel, 64

zucchini:
soup, creamy, 27
soupe au pistou, 28, *29*
summer *tian* with goat cheese and thyme, 166